CULTURES OF THE WORLD

Australia

mc **Marshall Cavendish**
Benchmark

New York

PICTURE CREDITS

Cover: © Andrew Watson/Getty Images
Andrew Watson/Lonely Planet Images: 114 • Cameron Spencer/Getty Images: 90 • Carl Court/AFP/Getty Images: 97 • Chris McGrath/Getty Images: 69 • Chris Mellor/Lonely Planet Images: 33, 74 • Christopher Groenhout/ Lonely Planet Images: 5 • Daniel Boag/Lonely Planet Images: 13 • David Wall/Lonely Planet Images: 7 • Dennis Jones/Lonely Planet Images: 113 • Diana Mayfield/Lonely Planet Images: 6, 47, 119 • Envision/Corbis: 130 • Fairfax Media/Getty Images: 28 • Feargus Cooney/Lonely Planet Images: 3, 11 • Gerard Walker/Lonely Planet Images: 112 • Gerti Deutsch/Getty Images: 94 • Getty Images: 10, 14, 18, 21, 25, 40, 43, 48, 49, 50, 52, 53, 59, 68, 103, 123, 125, 131 • Greg Elms/Lonely Planet Images: 64, 72 • Holger Leue/Lonely Planet Images: 20 • Hulton Archive/Getty Images: 107 • Ian Waldie/Bloomberg/Getty Images: 91 • Inmagine.com: 22, 23, 24, 39, 41, 42, 57, 58, 83, 87, 96, 104, 127 • Jamie McCarthy/WireImage/Getty Images: 100 • Jeremy Piper/Bloomberg/ Getty Images: 62 • John Banagan/Lonely Planet Images: 8 • John Sones/Lonely Planet Images: 122 • Johnny Haglund/Lonely Planet Images: 54 • Kristian Dowling/Getty Images: 60 • Krzysztof Dydynski/Lonely Planet Images: 79 • Lawrie Williams/Lonely Planet Images: 128 • Manfred Gottschalk/Lonely Planet Images: 9, 30, 31 • Mark Kolbe/Getty Images: 15 • Michael Coyne/Lonely Planet Images: 89, 115 • Michael Gebicki/Lonely Planet Images: 102 • Oliver Strewe/Lonely Planet Images: 38, 78, 80 • Orien Harvey/Lonely Planet Images: 84 • Patrick Eagar/Patrick Eagar Collection/Getty Images: 51 • Paul Crock/AFP/Getty Images: 85 • Paul Dymond/ Lonely Planet Images: 92 • Paul Kane/Getty Images: 109 • Peter Ptschelinzew/Lonely Planet Images: 82, 116 • Phil Weymouth/Lonely Planet Images: 117 • Quinn Rooney/Getty Images: 106 • Regis Martin/Lonely Planet Images: 76 • Richard Cummins/Lonely Planet Images: 75 • Richard I'Anson/Lonely Planet Images: 1, 12, 46, 67, 93, 118 • Ross Barnett/Lonely Planet Images: 70 • Saul Loeb/AFP/Getty Images: 34 • Sergio Dionisio/ Bloomberg/Getty Images: 36 • Simon Foale/Lonely Planet Images: 16 • The Sydney Morning Herald/Fairfax Media/Getty Images: 27 • Tom Cockrem/Lonely Planet Images: 56, 88 • Torsten Blackwood/AFP/Getty Images: 32, 71 • Wayne Walton/Lonely Planet Images: 77 • Will Salter/Lonley Planet Images: 65 • William West/AFP/ Getty Images: 105

PRECEDING PAGE
Portrait of a boy from the Juwulinypany community in the Kimberley region.

Publisher (U.S.): Michelle Bisson
Writers: Vijeya Rajendra, Sundran Rajendra, and Josie Elias
Editors: Deborah Grahame-Smith, Stephanie Pee
Copyreader: Tara Tomczyk
Designers: Nancy Sabato, Lynn Chin
Cover picture researcher: Tracey Engel
Picture researcher: Joshua Ang

Marshall Cavendish Benchmark
99 White Plains Road
Tarrytown, NY 10591
Website: www.marshallcavendish.us

Originated and designed by Times Media Private Limited
An imprint of Marshall Cavendish International (Asia) Private Limited
A member of Times Publishing Limited

Marshall Cavendish is a trademark of Times Publishing Limited.

Library of Congress Cataloging-in-Publication Data
Rajendra, Vijeya, 1936-
 Australia / Vijeya Rajendra, Sundran Rajendra, and Josie Elias. -- 3rd ed.
   p. ; cm. -- (Cultures of the world)
 ISBN 978-1-60870-990-8 (print) -- ISBN 978-1-60870-997-7 (eBook)
 1. Australia--Juvenile literature. I. Rajendra, Sundran, 1967- II. Elias, Josie III. Title.

DU96.R34 2013
994--dc23   2011042591

Printed in Malaysia
7 6 5 4 3 2 1

CONTENTS

AUSTRALIA TODAY

AUSTRALIA IS THE LAND "DOWN UNDER," AS THE ENTIRE continent lies below the equator in the Southern Hemisphere. Beyond kangaroos and koalas lies a vast continent of mystery and contradiction. From tropical rain forests to endless deserts, from golden beaches to ancient mountains, Australia is a land of flood and drought, heat and cold, fire and water. Australia is home to a number of animal and plant species, which are unique and found nowhere else on the planet. It is the most arid inhabited continent in the world. The interior has one of the lowest rainfalls in the world, and three-quarters of the land is either arid or semiarid and therefore very infertile.

In 2010 and 2011, Australia was hit by a slew of natural disasters. Queensland experienced extreme rainfall that caused heavy flooding, affecting more than 200,000 people in over 70 towns, including the city of Brisbane. The city of Victoria was also affected by flooding, partly caused by Cyclone Yasi, in early 2011. The floods damaged valuable farmland and destroyed crops and cattle. Damages were estimated to be about AUD$1 billion.

Crowds gather on East End Rundle Street in Adelaide for the Fringe Festival. Australia is home to about 21.7 million people.

The 21.7 million inhabitants of the continent of Australia live in one of the most cosmopolitan, highly urbanized states in the world. They live mostly on the coast or in major cities. Today this young nation, built on the heritage of the West, is preparing to play a greater political role among its neighbors in Asia. Australian multicultural society is made up of indigenous peoples and migrants who have come from around 200 different countries. It is an inclusive and liberal society, a nation built by people from diverse cultural backgrounds in Asia and Europe. The main language of Australia is English, but more than 4 million people speak a second language.

Australia boasts a spectacular environment, it is politically stable and economically strong, and the people are friendly and welcoming. It is not surprising that it is a very popular tourist destination. These qualities, combined with a well-developed education system, make it a very attractive place in which to live and work.

As a land of amazing and unique natural beauty, Australia is taking strict measures to conserve its fragile environment for future generations. Rich in natural resources, and with a strong global economy, Australia continues to attract great numbers of immigrants from all over the world. The Aboriginal and indigenous peoples are becoming more active in Australian society while preserving their traditional values, contributing their ancient heritage to Australia's young and multicultural society.

Australia is known for its diverse environment, ranging from beautiful azure waters and white sand beaches to harsh deserts.

GEOGRAPHY

A rock formation jutting out of the Southern Ocean in Port Campbell National Park. Formations like this are formed over years of erosion by wind and waves.

1

AUSTRALIA, THE SIXTH-LARGEST country in the world, lies in the Southern Hemisphere, between 11° and 44° south latitude and 113° and 154° east longitude.

Its population of 21.7 million inhabits an area of land about the same size as the continental United States. Mainland Australia, with an area of 2,988,902 square miles (7,741,220 square kilometers), is regarded as the world's seventh and smallest continent.

Australia has six states: Queensland (QLD), New South Wales (NSW), Victoria (VIC), Tasmania (TAS), South Australia (SA), and Western

The Buneroo Valley in South Australia.

Australia (WA). There are ten Australian territories outside the borders of the states—two mainland territories: Northern Territory (NT) and Australia Capital Territory (ACT); one offshore territory (Norfolk Island); and seven external territories (Jervis Bay Territory, Christmas Island, Cocos (Keeling) Islands, Coral Sea Islands, Ashmore and Cartier Islands, Territory of Heard Island and McDonald Islands, and Australian Antarctic Territory).

A LAND AS OLD AS TIME

The continent of Australia is often described as an "old land" because the geological activity that created the country's mountains, rivers, and plains ceased millions of years ago. Fortunately large earthquakes are rare in Australia; the last volcanic eruption in South Australia occurred at Mount Gambier 5,000 years ago. Over the centuries, wind and water have eroded the land's more spectacular features, leaving vast stretches of flat, featureless plains. The highest mountain in Australia, Mount Kosciuszko, is only 7,312 feet (2,229 meters) above sea level.

Mount Kosciuszko is the highest point in Australia.

Mount Kosciuszko lies in the southern part of the Eastern Highlands, a belt of elevated land stretching down the length of Australia's eastern coast from northern Queensland to central Victoria—a distance of 1,860 miles (2,993 km). Settlers first arriving in Australia called these highlands the Great Dividing Range since they were an obstacle blocking their exploration of the lands farther to the west.

Beyond the Great Dividing Range lie the great plains of the Central Lowlands. This area is remarkable for what lies beneath it—vast underground stores of water trapped in porous sandstone between beds of hard rock. Farmers use windmills to pump this water (called artesian water) to the surface to irrigate crops and water livestock.

Coastal sand dunes near Fowler's Bay in South Australia.

The western two-thirds of the Australian continent is an arid, flat surface called the Western Plateau. This ancient region, which is rich in minerals such as gold, nickel, cobalt, platinum, silver, palladium, lime, bauxite, and uranium, includes many deserts. One such desert is the 434-mile-wide (698-km-wide) Nullarbor Plain. Although it sounds like an Aboriginal name, the word *Nullarbor* is actually derived from the Latin *nullus arbor*, meaning "no tree," in reference to its treeless landscape. Travelers can cross the plain by car or on the Trans-Australian Railway, which has the longest stretch of straight railroad track in the world—298 miles (479 km).

CLIMATE

Because it spans both the tropical and temperate regions of the Southern Hemisphere, Australia experiences a variety of climates. The continent's desert interior gives way to tropical regions in the north. Bordering the desert is a dry region of semi-desert that acts as a transition zone to the

The Great Barrier Reef is a 132,819-square-mile (344,000-square-km) complex of islands and coral reefs stretching over 1,429 miles (2,300 km) along Australia's northeastern coast. Built by countless tiny coral polyps over a period of 2 million years, it is the largest known coral formation in the world. It was inscribed on the UNESCO World Heritage List in 1981.

Today the reef is one of the world's greatest tourist attractions and provides spectacular scenery. It contains mangroves, sea grass, muddy and sandy seabed communities, inter-reefal areas, and deep oceanic waters. It is home to about 1,500 species of fish, 400 species of hard reef-building corals, more than 1,500 species of sponges, and more than 4,000 mollusks. The sea grass beds and reefs are the feeding grounds for dugongs and turtles, many of which are endangered.

For many years the crown of thorns starfish (COTS), known scientifically as Acanthaster planci, was believed to be destroying the reef. Recent research has shown that this starfish prefers to eat the faster-growing and more common species of coral. These include large, flat plate corals and branching staghorn corals. By eating these, the starfish may help the slower-growing corals compete for space on the reef. When hard coral runs out, the COTS will eat soft corals, algae clams, and sea anemones. A small crab, Trapezia cymdoce, protects the coral Pocillopora damicornis from being preyed upon by crown of thorns sea stars by breaking their spines off.

more humid regions of the north, east, and south. The southeastern coast, where most of Australia's population lives, is cooler and drier. In the south of the country, temperatures drop considerably in the winter and frosts are common. During the winter months of June, July, and August, snow falls in the Eastern Highlands of Victoria and New South Wales. The southwest is very hot and dry in the summer, but milder and wetter in the winter. The climate is similar to that of the Mediterranean countries of Europe, or of California in the United States.

Summers in Australia range from hot to very hot, with temperatures soaring to over 104°F (40°C) during the summer months, which last from December to February in the Southern Hemisphere. Because of the heat and lack of rain, bushfires often rage through the landscape, destroying an average of 780 square miles (2,020 square km) of forest every year. Between January 2006 and February 2011, an area of 7,122 square miles (18,445 square km) burned in major bushfires, resulting in 180 deaths and more than 4,000 properties damaged or destroyed.

The snow-covered mountainside of Mount Hotham.

Severe Tropical Cyclone Yasi—the first category 5 storm to hit the Australian coast since 1918—devastated a series of small towns in north Queensland after crossing the coast near Mission Beach, south of Cairns, on February 3, 2011. Significant wind damage to structures and vegetation resulted in mass devastation. Buildings were ripped apart, power poles torn down, and crops and large trees uprooted. Telecommunications were cut, and more than 175,000 homes had no electricity. At its height the cyclone covered an area bigger than Italy or New Zealand.

Cyclone Yasi and floods have been responsible for the devastation of the sea grass beds of the Great Barrier Reef on which the green sea turtle feeds. As a result the turtles are starving. Reef HQ in Cairns is home to a turtle hospital, where some of the sick turtles are brought for medical treatment and rehabilitation.

RAINFALL The high temperatures and low rainfall of the inland areas mean that 70 percent of Australia receives less than 20 inches (50 centimeters) of rain a year, making it the world's driest inhabited continent. Farming in

A storm brewing over farmland in Deloraine in Tasmania.

Queensland suffered extreme flooding from December 2010 to January 2011. More than 200,000 people across 70 towns were affected.

these areas is difficult, but not always impossible, thanks to the exploitation of artesian water and the construction of many irrigation projects. In contrast the east, the southwestern tip, and the tropical regions in the north are wetter. Cairns, a town on the northern coast of Queensland, receives an average annual rainfall of 78 inches (199 cm). Tully, slightly south of Cairns, has Australia's highest annual rainfall—126 inches (320 cm).

In most areas of Australia, there are wide changes in rainfall from year to year. Significant flooding occurred in many areas of Victoria and Queensland during late December 2010 and January 2011, with three-quarters of Queensland declared a disaster zone. These floods caused loss of life; damage to infrastructure, public and private property; destruction of crops; and loss of livestock and deterioration of health due to waterborne diseases. Droughts are common in the inland areas and may last for several years.

The strange-looking platypus can only be found in Australia.

NATIVE ANIMALS

When the first Europeans arrived in Australia and started to explore the country, they could hardly believe the strange animals they saw. They, and the settlers who came after them, were especially fascinated by the various types of marsupials that they saw in Australia. Marsupials are mammals that raise their offspring in a pouch on their body until the youngsters are a reasonable size and can fend for themselves. These creatures have adapted to the harsh Australian environment. The marsupial family includes possums, koalas, kangaroos, wombats, and carnivores such as the fierce Tasmanian devil (*Sarcophilus harrisii*).

Kangaroos are a common sight in the Australian countryside, or bush. Like other marsupials, female kangaroos carry their babies, called joeys, in a pouch located on their abdomen. Kangaroos move by hopping on their powerful hind legs. They can leap distances as far as 30 feet (9 m) in a single effort. When fighting, kangaroos lash out with their hind legs or punch with their smaller front paws. One kangaroo that escaped from a zoo in Adelaide knocked out a policeman with one punch before it was recaptured!

UNIQUE CREATURES Unlike the kangaroo, which feeds on grass, the koala, another marsupial, only eats the leaves of the eucalyptus. Koalas spend most of their lives clinging to tree branches, where they will sleep for up to 18 hours a day. When they are old enough to leave the pouch, koalas catch a ride on their mother's back. Koalas appear to be shy, cuddly creatures, but they have sharp claws.

The most unusual creature of the bush is the duck-billed platypus (*Ornithorhynchus anatinus*). The platypus is one of two animals, the other being the echidna, in a group of animals unique to Australia—the monotremes.

Inside the museum in Eden, a fishing town in New South Wales, is the skeleton of Old Tom, a killer whale, or orca (Orcinus Orca), that formed an extraordinary partnership with local fishermen in the 19th century. These fishermen hunted whalebone whales, which migrated along Australia's eastern coast during winter.

Whenever a whale strayed close to Eden, Old Tom and his pack herded it into the town's bay. If no fishermen were around, some of the pack went to the shore and raised a terrific noise. The fishermen quickly recognized the signal to rush to their boats. While they were hurrying out, the orcas attacked the unfortunate whale. By the time the fishermen arrived, the whale was battered and exhausted and was easily killed. In return for their help, the fishermen allowed the killer pack to drag the dead whale to the sea bottom, where they feasted on the tongue and lips. A few days later the dead whale would float to the surface and the fishermen returned to tow the rest of the body to shore.

This bizarre partnership lasted nearly 90 years. But after World War I, the orcas started to disappear. They were killed at sea by Norwegian sailors fishing off the coast. Once the killer whales were gone, the whalebone whales stopped coming into Eden. The town's whaling industry closed down. In 1930 Old Tom, by then well over 90 years old, made his last visit to Eden. The next day he was found dead, drifting in the bay. Local fishermen, who recognized their old friend, dragged his body to shore. The skeleton was sent to the town's museum, where it remains on display to this day.

These are mammals that lay eggs and produce milk for their young. The platypus's body is covered with fur like that of other mammals, but it has a bill and webbed feet like a duck's.

Another remarkable animal is the mallee fowl (*Leipoa ocellata*), which builds its nest out of a mound of dirt. The female covers its eggs with dirt and keeps them at a constant temperature by adding or removing dirt.

The largest bird native to Australia is the emu (*Dromaius novaehollandiae*). The emu belongs to a group of flightless running birds with flat breastbones known as ratites. Its typical diet consists of seeds, fruits, insects, and the

new shoots of plants. The emu is unusual in that the male incubates the eggs for a period of 7 to 8 weeks.

Australia has several highly dangerous native animals. The venom of the tiger snake (*Notechis scutatus*) of southern and eastern Australia is so deadly that one drop can kill a person. The bite of the tiny red-back spider (*Latrodectus hasselti*) is also highly toxic. It makes its home in sheltered nooks and crannies, and has even been discovered under the toilet seat in bathrooms in the bush!

Australia is home to the tiger snake, one of the deadliest snakes in the world.

NATIVE VEGETATION

Australia's coastal regions boast the most luxuriant vegetation. A major physical feature of the continent is the chain of mountain ranges, which runs just inland from the southern and eastern coast. From the height of these ranges to the coast lie Australia's heaviest forests. A second great forest belt also stretches 350 miles (563 km) through southwestern Western Australia.

In the north, these forests are typically monsoon rain forests, similar to the forests of Indonesia and Malaysia. Queensland and the northeastern parts of Cape York Peninsula exhibit the most exotic vegetation, including tropical rain forest, eucalypt forests, wetlands, and mangrove forests. In the cooler south, there are coastal and mallee woodlands and cool temperature rain forests. Mallee-form trees include bull mallee (*Eucalyptus behriana*), red mallee (*E. calycogona*), oil mallee (*E. oleosa*), and dumosa mallee (*E. dumosa*).

Forests found in the corner of southwestern Australia are rich in vegetation, and many of the plants found here are unique to Western Australia. The four dominant tree species are jarrah, karri, tingle, and tuart.

The forest in Tasmania is known as cool temperate rain forest. This grows in areas with more than 47 inches (120 cm) of annual rainfall. The dominant tree species are myrtle (*Nothofagus cunninghamii*), celery-top pine (*Phyllocladus asplendiifolius*), leatherwood (*Eucryphia lucida*), sassafras (*Atherosperma moschatum*), huon pine (*Lagarostrobos franklinii*), king billy pine (*Athrotaxis selaginoides*), and deciduous beech (*Nothofagus gunnii*). Inland, as the climate becomes more arid, the forests are replaced by shrublands. This includes small areas of coastal heathland and vast regions of saltbush and bluebush, with scattered low acacias or eucalyptus trees, savannah woodlands, and grasslands.

Australia's national flower is the golden wattle (*Acacia pycnantha*), which produces large clusters of tiny golden flowers. Another striking plant is the Illawarra flame tree (*Brachychiton acerifolius*) of the coastal rain forests on the Eastern Highlands. From a distance, its bright red flowers create the illusion that the tree is on fire.

INTERNET LINKS

http://australian-animals.net/

This website provides an alphabetical listing of Australian animals, birds, and mammals, including links to photographs, descriptions, habitat, social habits, and breeding.

http://rainforest-australia.com

This website specializes in the "Wet Tropics" of Northeastern Australia, including links, photographs, and detailed information on the flora and fauna.

www.killersofeden.com/index.htm

This site is dedicated to the Killers of Eden, the fascinating and true story of the killer whales of Twofold Bay.

HISTORY

2

A USTRALIA'S INDIGENOUS PEOPLE probably migrated to Australia from Southeast Asia between 40,000 and 70,000 years ago. At that time Australia was still joined to the continent of Asia by a string of small islands.

Sailing south in canoes, the migrants landed on the northern coast of Australia and then moved southward across the rest of the new land. Europeans who came to Australia later called the original settlers *Aborigines*, meaning "indigenous inhabitants."

By the time the first British colonists arrived in Australia at Botany Bay in 1788, the population of the Aborigines had grown to about

Australia's history can be traced back to the ancient times of Gondwanaland when the continents were joined together, to the dinosaurs, the Aborigines, right through to the colonization of the country by the English, the World Wars, and the modern era.

British colonists first landed in Australia at Botany Bay.

300,000. Nevertheless the British colonists declared the land *terra nullius*, meaning "land uninhabited by humans"!

NOMADS

The Aborigines were seminomadic hunter-gatherers living in family clans, each with its own territory where clan members could camp, hunt, and fish. These territories or "traditional lands" were defined by geographic boundaries such as mountains, lakes, or rivers. The clans burned large tracts of forest to provide grazing land for giant kangaroos and other animals that are now extinct; these were killed and eaten. The Aboriginal hunters brought two useful aids from their original homeland—the dingo, a hunting dog that could not bark; and the returning boomerang. This V-shaped wooden device has two airfoil wings arranged so that, when thrown correctly, the spinning creates unbalanced aerodynamic forces that makes it travel in an elliptical

A young Aboriginal boy with a boomerang.

path and return to its point of origin. The boomerang was used mostly by Australian Aborigines to hunt animals.

Aborigines were very effective hunters. The secret of their success lay in their wise use of natural resources. They occupied land in a productive way, moving on with climatic changes and in response to environmental demands. Today their methods of finding food and water are taught to soldiers, to help them survive in Australia's inhospitable interior. Although they did not build permanent settlements or carry many possessions, the Aborigines recorded their history and culture in paintings on rocks and caves using charcoal, clay, and ocher. Archaeologists have also found evidence of regular contact between Aboriginal hunters and Indonesian traders from the north.

Plaque on a monument indicating the landing point of Captain James Cook.

TERRA AUSTRALIS INCOGNITA

For many thousands of years, the Aborigines were the only people to visit and live in Australia. Europeans, however, suspected that a "great southern land" existed. Such a land, they reasoned, was needed to balance the weight of the land in the Northern Hemisphere and prevent the world from tipping over! This land was called *Terra Australis Incognita*, a Greek phrase meaning the "unknown southern land." This phrase was first used by the Egyptian geographer Ptolemy who, in the second century, sketched a map of the known coasts of Asia and a big unknown piece of land to the south.

Seventeenth-century Dutch merchants sailing the trade routes to the East Indies were the first Europeans to set foot in Australia. When the British learned of their reports, they were keen to claim the land for themselves.

A statue of Captain James Cook in Hyde Park in Sydney.

In 1768 they sent a man on a secret mission. The man's name was James Cook. Publicly he was preparing to visit Tahiti to observe the planet Venus. But Cook had secret orders to find the southern land and claim it for England. He first sighted Australia on April 20, 1770. He spent about four months mapping the eastern coast, describing the flora and fauna, and attempting to make contact with the natives, the Aborigines.

SETTLING IN

Although news of Cook's voyage caused a sensation in London, more than 10 years passed before the government decided to establish a colony in Australia. It was to be a penal colony. At that time Britain had a serious crime problem. The government decided to reduce overcrowding in British jails by sending convicts to Australia. This system was known as transportation.

The first colony was set up in Sydney Cove in 1788. In the beginning, life was very hard for the new settlers. Their crops did not do well. Their cattle were stolen by the Aborigines, and food had to be rationed.

Nevertheless conditions gradually improved and the colony grew. Other settlements were built along the coast of New South Wales and in Tasmania. Between 1788 and 1868, about 160,000 convicts were sent to Australia. The first free settlers did not arrive until 1793. These people chose to escape poverty and unemployment in Georgian England and take their chances in Australia. The new migrants increased the status of the colony and encouraged the growth of industry and farming.

By 1859 five colonies had grown along the coast of Australia: New South Wales, Tasmania, Queensland, Victoria, and South Australia. Each colony

A photograph, taken around 1932, of children leaving Waterloo in Britain for Western Australia to undergo training at a farm school.

Forceful measures were taken by white settlers in their quest for development. Tribes, clans, and families were dispersed by the land grab.

had its own governor, laws, trade policies, police, and transportation system. Relations among the colonies were not good. A fierce rivalry existed among the older colonies, and very few people ever visited other colonies.

Australia's vast inland had scarcely been mapped. A number of explorers, some sent by the colonial authorities, set about finding out what lay within the country's enormous interior. The men chosen for these expeditions had to be brave and persevering. They had to travel for months in desolate, unknown country, had to repel attacks from hostile Aborigines, and had somehow to find their way back home. Understandably many of these men never returned.

THE SQUATTERS

Settlers took advantage of the new lands opened up by explorers. They brought flocks of sheep and drove them inland to graze on the newly discovered grasslands. Since these farmers did not buy the land they used, but instead declared their claim to the government, they were called squatters. Squatting was far from easy. Besides the constant threats of

Stealing a buckle or a loaf of bread was enough for a person to be sentenced to a life of exile in a penal settlement such as Port Arthur in Tasmania. Thus Australia became a dumping ground for petty thieves, Irish rebels, and prostitutes.

drought, bushfires, and floods, squatters had to deal with attacks from the Aborigines and armed robbers called bushrangers. Their success depended on how many workers they could hire and on the fluctuating price of wool in London. Worse than all this was the isolation. Loneliness and boredom sent many men back to the towns to find a bride. The wives of squatters faced a tough life. They had to endure poverty, isolation, and danger. Supplies and mail, often brought by ox wagons, came a few times a year, if the weather allowed. Women who could not shoot a gun or ride a horse were scorned and were at a real disadvantage when it came to fending off attacks by Aborigines.

CLASHES WITH THE ABORIGINES Fighting between the Aborigines and white settlers became increasingly common. The squatters had taken over the Aborigines' traditional hunting lands. Their seminomadic way of life was disrupted and would never again be the same. Since they were unable to get their food in the traditional way, the Aborigines fought back by stealing the squatters' sheep. They also attacked the squatters' homes and families. The squatters in turn killed whole tribes of Aboriginal men, women, and children. A century after the First Fleet (the fleet of ships that transported the first British settlers to Australia) arrived in Australia, the Aboriginal population had been reduced from 300,000 to 80,000.

BUDDING NATION

On the first day of the 20th century, the states put aside their differences and joined to form the Commonwealth of Australia. Federation and nationhood for the six colonies were not a revolt against the old order, but rather a coming-of-age.

However, like many other countries in the first half of the 20th century, the new nation soon found itself face-to-face with the double burden of war and depression.

Australia, as a member of the British Empire, automatically followed Great Britain's declaration of war on Germany in 1914. Over the next four years, more than 330,000 Australian men volunteered for service in Europe, the Middle East, New Guinea, and the Indian Ocean. On April 25, 1915, Australian soldiers took part in their most famous battle: the Gallipoli campaign. Masterminded by British prime minister Winston Churchill and involving Australian and New Zealand Army Corps (ANZACs), it proved to be a disaster from the very beginning. Australians, however, commemorate the battle every year on ANZAC Day, the day when Australians first fought for their new nation. A source of pride to their countrymen, the ANZACs are remembered by Australians as "the finest body of men brought together in modern times."

An Australian soldier at Woolloomooloo in Sydney, preparing to leave for the war in 1915.

Elizabeth Beckford, age 70, was sentenced to seven years' transportation in 1787 for stealing 11 pounds (5 kilograms) of cheese. James Freeman was condemned to death for robbery when he was 16 years old; the sentence was later changed to seven years' transportation. James Grace was just 11 years old when he was sentenced to seven years' transportation in 1792; he had been caught stealing a pair of silk stockings.

Construction of the Sydney Harbour Bridge in 1925.

LAND OF OPPORTUNITY

After World War I, Australia opened its doors to emigrants from Britain and Europe. For the next 50 years, immigrants came to Australia in large numbers. New labor and new markets made the country rich in the 1920s. This period of prosperity ended in 1929 when Australia, along with the United States and many other countries, was affected by the worldwide economic depression. One of the few bright spots during those years was the opening of Sydney's famous Harbour Bridge in 1932. Work on the bridge had started nearly a decade earlier. Over the years Sydney's inhabitants looked on in wonder as the huge single arch was slowly completed. Despite the hard times, more than 350,000 people flocked to Sydney to catch a glimpse of the bridge when it was declared open.

World War II, which began in 1939, resulted in closer relations between the United States and Australia. After losing the Philippines to Japanese forces, the United States set up its Pacific base in Australia. One million troops were stationed in Melbourne and Brisbane between 1942 and 1945. Many Australians believe it was the U.S. army presence that prevented Australia from being invaded by the Japanese. Twenty years after World War II, Australian and American soldiers fought together in the Vietnam War in the belief that the spread of communism had to be stopped. Soldiers returning from this controversial war were often booed by crowds. Vietnam War veterans are still recognized and honored in Australia. In recent years Australia's attitude toward communist countries has relaxed. In fact, Australia was the first Western nation to officially recognize the People's Republic of China. Many Australian goods are sold to China and the former Soviet Union. Presently Australia is trying to create closer cultural and economic ties with its neighbors, particularly Southeast Asia and the Pacific Islands. The government spends millions of dollars on foreign aid to countries, such as the Philippines and Indonesia. Nevertheless Australia still maintains a strong relationship with the United States as well as its traditional ties with Britain.

In 1988 Australia celebrated its bicentenary—the 200th anniversary of the arrival of the First Fleet. The World Expo was held in Brisbane that year. In 2000 Sydney hosted the Olympic Games. In 2006 the Commonwealth Games were hosted in Melbourne. Australians are aware of how much they have accomplished in the past and how much still lies ahead.

INTERNET LINKS

http://adb.anu.edu.au/biography/cook-james-1917

This Web site includes concise, informative, and fascinating descriptions of the lives of more than 12,000 significant and representative persons in Australian history. A comprehensive biography of Captain James Cook can also be found on this site.

http://australia.gov.au/about-australia

This site furnishes a brief overview of the country and the government.

www.australianhistory.org/

This website provides information on the history of Australia from ancient history to modern times. This site also has a section on Australian information that includes statistics, slang, and fun facts.

www.embraceaustralia.com/culture/aboriginal-australia/

This website covers Aboriginal history and includes a time line with further information on indigenous Australians.

GOVERNMENT

Parliament House in Australia's capital of Canberra.

3

THE COMMONWEALTH OF Australia was formed in 1901 when six independent British colonies joined to become states of a new nation.

The rules of government were enshrined in the Australian Constitution, which defined how the Australian government would operate and on what issues it could pass laws. The six state parliaments retain the power to pass laws related to any matter not controlled by the Commonwealth under Section 51 of the Australian Constitution. The British monarchy is represented in Australia by a governor-general and six state governors. The head of each state government is known as the premier.

Australia's formal name is the Commonwealth of Australia. The form of government used is a constitutional monarchy—"constitutional" because the procedures and powers of the Australian government are defined by a written constitution, and "monarchy" because Australia's head of state is Queen Elizabeth II of England.

The Senate chamber in Australia's Parliament House.

FEDERAL GOVERNMENT

Power rests with the elected political party that holds the majority in the House of Representatives. The leader is the prime minister. Government is modeled on the British system of two governing bodies: a legislative assembly (the House of Representatives) and a council of review (the Senate). The Senate consists of 76 members who are elected every six years. The House of Representatives has 150 members and they face elections every three years.

Although Australia's constitution gives the House of Representatives the right to enact laws, they must be passed by a majority in the Senate before they become law. Additionally any laws that involve changes to the constitution must be decided by a referendum in which the country's citizens vote on whether or not they want such changes to take place. History has

Australian Prime Minister Julia Gillard (*center, in white*) with her cabinet of ministers.

The national flag consists of a small Union Jack, representing Australia's historical link with Britain; the five stars of the Southern Cross constellation (a prominent feature of the night sky in the Southern Hemisphere); and the seven-pointed star, which represents Australia's six states and its group of territories. The Australian Red Ensign, a red version of the national flag, is the only flag allowable for merchant ships registered in Australia. The national coat of arms consists of a shield divided into six sections, each containing a state badge, surrounded by an ermine border, signifying the federation of the states into one nation. The shield is supported by two native animals—an emu on the right, and a kangaroo, Australia's national animal emblem, on the left. These two animals were chosen for the coat of arms because neither can move backward, thus symbolizing the eternal progress of the nation. They are resting on a branch of golden wattle (Acacia pycnantha Benth), Australia's floral emblem.

On July 14, 1995, the Australian Aboriginal flag and the Torres Strait Islander flag were proclaimed additional official flags of Australia under the Flags Act.

Julia Gillard is Australia's first woman prime minister. She was elected in 2010.

shown that Australians are not eager to alter the constitution that has served them so well—of the 42 proposals put to a vote in 18 referenda, only 8 have been passed.

THE REGIONAL LEVEL

Each of Australia's states is administered by a parliament, which consists of a legislative council (similar to the federal Senate) and a legislative assembly (similar to the House of Representatives). The premier is the leader of the political party dominating the legislative assembly. State parliaments existed long before the creation of the federal government in 1901 and, therefore, retain many of their former powers. In addition to collecting state taxes and duties, each state runs schools and hospitals, administers its own laws, and has its own police force.

POLITICAL PARTIES

There are four major political parties in Australia.

THE AUSTRALIAN LABOUR PARTY *(ALP) is a social democratic party, which was started in 1891 by sheep shearers who were unhappy with their pay and working conditions. As the party of the working people, it has a strong tradition of democratic socialism, pioneering reforms such as pensions and minimum wages. Kevin Rudd was Australia's 26th prime minister and the 19th leader of the ALP. He served from December 3, 2007, until June 24, 2010, when he was replaced as leader of the Parliamentary Labour Party by the first woman to hold office of prime minister, Julia Gillard. The Parliamentary Labour Party refers to those people who are members of the Labour Party and who have been elected to the House of Representatives and are therefore members of Parliament.*

THE LIBERAL PARTY OF AUSTRALIA *After its founding in 1944, this center-right party dominated federal politics for two decades. Liberals believe in free enterprise and the freedom to conduct their lives with minimal government interference. To this end, they support the reduction of taxes and restrictions on trade and business. On March 2, 1996, a coalition between the Liberal Party and the National Party won the federal election, ending 13 years of Labour Party government. John Howard then became the prime minister. He served from March 1996 until December 3, 2007.*

THE NATIONAL PARTY OF AUSTRALIA *Known as the National Country Party at the time of its creation in 1919, it is the champion of primary industries such as farming and mining. The party draws its membership mainly from Australia's rural population. Since 1949 the National Party and Liberal Party have combined forces in both state and federal parliaments to form ruling coalitions.*

THE AUSTRALIAN DEMOCRATS *Formed in 1977 by Don Chipp, this party was set up to keep a check on the other major parties, or, in the more colorful words of Senator Chipp, "to keep the b*st*rds honest."*

Voters casting their votes in the 2010 national elections.

Cities and shires (counties) are governed by local councils headed by mayors. The local council's responsibilities include town planning, waste management, and road construction.

PARTICIPATING IN A DEMOCRACY

Australia has a short but strong tradition of democracy. Since members of all levels of government are elected by the people, most citizens find themselves visiting a voting booth at least once a year. Unlike in other democracies, including the United States, Britain, and France, voting in Australia is compulsory for all adults 18 years old and above. Citizens who are overseas or otherwise unable to vote in person at a polling center for which they are enrolled are required to mail in an absentee vote. Those who do not vote are fined.

All elections held in Australia use a procedure known as the preferential voting system, in which voters assign an order to each candidate. The candidate of their choice would be first, followed by their second choice, and so on. Because of this detailed procedure, it takes several days to count all the votes. After an election, members of the ruling party elect a prime minister or, in the case of a state, a premier, who then appoints a cabinet of ministers, each responsible for a particular area of government, such as defense, education, or welfare.

THE REPUBLICAN DEBATE

Australians' desire for a republic seems to be growing, especially among the young. The Australian Republican Movement (ARM) argues that changes to the constitution and the Australian system of democracy should be minimal. Severing ties with the Commonwealth is also not favored by the ARM.

Opinion polls have shown that although the majority of Australians are in favor of a republic (as opposed to constitutional monarchy), they are not in favor of adopting the U.S. or French systems. However, the final step toward complete self-government failed when Australians rejected the November 1999 referendum to make Australia a republic with an Australian head of state. Queen Elizabeth II, head of state of the United Kingdom, continues to be Australia's head of state.

INTERNET LINKS

http://primeministers.naa.gov.au/

This site provides information on the National Archives of Australia and includes profiles of Australia's 27 prime ministers.

www.nla.gov.au/oz/gov/

This website provides information on the National Library of Australia. It also presents information and links to general sites for researching the Australian government on the Internet.

ECONOMY

Grapevines at a vineyard in Mudgee in New South Wales.

4

USTRALIANS HAVE TRADITIONALLY relied on exports to maintain one of the highest standards of living in the world. Australia is the world's leading supplier of several important commodities, such as aluminum, wool, beef and veal, coal, mineral sands, live goats and sheep, and refined lead.

An old saying went that Australia's economic fortunes "ride on the sheep's back," in reference to the fact that the nation has relied on the export of primary resources, such as sheep, cattle, and minerals,

A sheep shearer expertly and quickly shears wool off a sheep at an agricultural show.

Australia has become an internationally competitive, advanced market economy. In the 1990s it boasted one of the fastest-growing economies in the Organisation for Economic Co-operation and Development (OECD). This performance was primarily due to economic reforms adopted in the 1980s. The economy grew by 1.2 percent during 2009, the best performance in the OECD, and by 3.3 percent in 2010.

Australian ranchers herding cattle into pens. Australia is a large exporter of beef.

to create wealth. Australia is the world's largest producer of greasy wool, producing 21 to 5 percent of the world's greasy wool in 2008. Production for 2010 and 2011 was estimated at 771 million pounds (350 million kg) of greasy wool from 75 million sheep.

Australia's diverse and abundant natural resources include iron ore, coal, gold, natural gas, uranium, and renewable energy sources. These attract high levels of foreign investment. In addition to having a large services sector, Australia is also a significant exporter of food, natural resources, and energy. The Gillard government is focusing on increasing Australia's economic productivity to ensure the sustainability of growth. Australia is engaged in the Trans-Pacific Partnership talks and negotiating free trade agreements with Japan, China, and Korea.

Long referred to as the "lucky country" because of its natural wealth, Australia is aiming to become, through the hard work and ingenious efforts of its people, the "clever country."

TRADE PARTNERS

Australia trades with both developed and developing nations. In 2009 China was its biggest customer, buying 21.8 percent of all Australian exports. Australia's major exports to China are minerals, fuels, and agricultural products. Another close trading partner is Japan, which accounts for 19.2 percent of Australia's exports. China and the United States are Australia's largest suppliers, usually of capital equipment. Products from these two countries make up nearly a third of all Australian imports.

MINERALS AND ENERGY

Australia is a land of incredible mineral wealth. Its deposits of coal, which can satisfy the demands of the whole world for several centuries, is the nation's single largest export earner, representing about 23 percent of Australia's total exports of goods and services in 2008 to 2009. Australia is the world's largest producer of aluminum, most of which is mined along the western coast of the Cape York Peninsula, and the second largest exporter of iron ore. Alumina, lead, zinc, diamonds, gold, and silver are also mined in

A gold mine in Kalgoorlie, Western Australia.

Ninety-five percent of the opals and half of the sapphires that reach the world's markets come from Australia. The world's largest opal mine is near Coober Pedy, a town in South Australia. Because temperatures in the district often exceed 104°F (40°C), many of the townspeople live in underground homes dug into the dry earth. The Argyle Diamond Mine (above) in the East Kimberley region of Western Australia produces most of the world's diamonds.

Gold has been mined in great quantities in the states of Victoria, Queensland, Western Australia, and New South Wales since the gold rushes of the 1850s. A number of massive nuggets have been found: The world's largest single mass of gold is strictly speaking not a nugget; it is a specimen known as a matrix. However, it was a single mass of gold and weighed an estimated 187.5 pounds (85.04 kg). It is known as the Beyers and Hotermann Specimen, after the people who found it. The 156-pound (71.01-kg) Welcome Stranger nugget was found on June 9, 1858, at Bakery Hill, Ballarat, Victoria.

In 1931 the body of Harold Lasseter was found in the Northern Territory. Lasseter had earlier claimed to have found a fabulous mile-long (1.6-km-long) reef of gold. Although a number of adventurers have tried and failed to find Lasseter's Reef, it is widely believed that the reef and its incredible wealth do exist, and are waiting somewhere in the outback to be found.

substantial quantities, along with natural gas, uranium, titanium, zircon, rutile, ilmenite, and gold. The income earned from minerals, metals, and fuels accounts for 50 percent of export earnings. In 2008 to 2009 Australia maintained its position as the world's largest coal exporter, with exports of 261 million tons (237 million metric tons), or 28 percent of the world total. Still it is estimated that only a tiny amount of the continent's vast reserves has so far been mined.

Workers handpicking grapes at a vineyard in Hunter Valley in New South Wales.

AGRICULTURE

Despite Australia's mostly arid soil and dry climate, agricultural exports, including wheat, wool, beef, sugar, and dairy products, earn approximately a third of Australia's national income. This success is in part due to limited domestic demand because of the nation's small population and the application of sophisticated farming techniques to semiarid lands. Sheep ranches, known as stations, in Australia's inland stock 12 head of sheep for every square mile. Such stations are tens of thousands of acres in size. Most of Australia's 145 million sheep are raised for their wool.

Because of Australia's unpredictable climate and the continual fluctuation in international demand for agricultural products, the volume and value of Australia's agricultural produce vary greatly from year to year. The nation's farmers cope with the variable market by rapidly changing to new crops and livestock as the need arises. In 1999 the agricultural sector was favored by strong domestic demand, low interest rates, and low inflation. Significant flooding occurred in many areas of Queensland during late December 2010 and early January 2011, with three-quarters of the state declared a disaster zone. This was followed by Cyclone Yasi and then severe floods in Victoria. These natural disasters devastated crops, especially bananas and sugarcane, with many of the plantations completely destroyed.

MANUFACTURING

In addition to its steel works and aluminum smelters, Australia's major manufacturing industries include clothing and textiles, chemicals, aeronautical equipment, and electronics. In 2009 Australia produced 225,713 cars. Four of the largest international motor vehicle makers—Ford, General Motors, Mitsubishi, and Toyota—have factories in Australia.

TOURISM

In recent years, Australia has been riding the crest of an unprecedented wave of popularity among international travelers. In 2009 a total of 5,584,000 tourists visited Australia. Tourism is one of the largest industries in Australia, and in 2010 it provided 776,024 jobs in the accommodation and food services sector. There were 5.9 million visitors to Australia between May 2010 and May 2011. In the month of May 2011 alone there were 386,600 visitors. Of these 94,500 came from New Zealand, 39,400 came from the Americas, 30,300 came from China, 26,000 came from the United Kingdom, 22,700 from Singapore, and 18,400 from Japan. Visitors also came in significant numbers from Malaysia, India, Indonesia, Thailand, Korea, Hong Kong, Taiwan, Germany, and France.

INTERNET LINKS

https://www.cia.gov/library/publications/the-world-factbook/geos/as.html

This website provides detailed information on the geography, economy, government, and people of Australia, including transportation, communications, and transnational issues.

www.argylediamonds.com.au/

The Argyle Diamond website provides an insight into the history and operation of their open-pit mine to the construction of their underground mine. It includes photos, videos, and lots of interesting information.

www.opalcapitaloftheworld.com.au/

Detailed information on the opal-mining town of Coober Pedy and surrounding areas is included in this website.

www.wool.com/Media-Centre_Australian-Wool-Production.htm

This comprehensive website provides detailed information on many aspects of wool production from the health and well-being of the sheep to dyeing and finishing the wool.

ENVIRONMENT

Beauchamp Falls in Great Otway National Park.

G

REETED BY A VAST AND OLD continent, Australia's early settlers must have felt that the land was inexhaustible and unalterable.

But unfortunately 200 years of uncontrolled hunting and land clearing as well as water and air pollution have caused the destruction of unique ecosystems and the extinction of many plants and animals, fundamentally changing the face of Australia's landscape. The country is committed to conserving its natural heritage and has a range of protection procedures in place, including the reduction of greenhouse gas emissions.

Rock formations formed over years of wind erosion at Gantheaume Point in Western Australia.

5

Australia's environment, productive land, and natural icons are fundamental to its national identity. Much of the country's wealth comes from the environment through agriculture and tourism. The Australian government is investing millions of dollars to achieve a real and measurable difference to Australia's environment by funding projects that improve biodiversity and sustainable farming practices.

THE THREAT TO BIODIVERSITY

Biodiversity, or biological diversity, refers to the variety of plants and animals found in a specific area. Australia has an extraordinarily high number of species of plants and animals, and many of them are unique to the country. This biodiversity is under threat. Already 14 of the original marsupial species are extinct, among them the Tasmanian tiger (*Thylacinus potens*). Thylacines were doglike marsupial carnivores whose last representative, the Tasmanian "tiger," became extinct in the last century. Fossil records show that an additional 13 marsupials are now extinct. Seven species of rodents have become extinct since European settlement, including hopping-mice (*Notomys longicaudatus*), one tree rat, and one stick-nest rat. A further dozen species are under threat due to loss of habitat. One-third of Australia's native mammals have become extinct since European settlement, and one-half of these were rodents. Many other native mammals are currently threatened with extinction, including the dugong (*Dugong dugon*), which

The now-extinct Tasmanian tiger was only found in Australia.

The Australian cassowary is a protected species.

is now a protected species in Australia. The Tasmanian bettong (*Bettongia gaimadi*) is only found in the eastern half of Tasmania. It became extinct on mainland Australia in the early part of the 20th century largely because of land clearance projects and loss of habitat. It remains moderately common in suitable habitats, but is wholly protected. The long-footed potoroo (*Potorous longipes*) is a forest-dwelling rat kangaroo and is listed as an endangered species.

The status of threatened and non-threatened birds has improved, but more species are in decline today than in 2003. Where active management is undertaken, success is more prominent than failure in improving the state of bird populations. Eighty-one taxa (species and subspecies) were identified as "near threatened" in 2000. The Bush Stone-curlew is still widespread in northern Australia, where it has few predators, but throughout southeastern Australia it is now locally extinct in several districts and is listed as "rare" in South Australia and "endangered" in New South Wales and Victoria. There have been significant changes in the way native vegetation is managed during the 200 years of European occupation. Land clearance for agriculture and urban development; the introduction of weeds, diseases, and feral animals; changed drought and flood patterns; and altered fire and grazing patterns have affected the survival of many species. More than 1,180 Australian plant species are endangered and more than 60 species are thought to be extinct.

A further threat to Australia's biodiversity is mining. The country's mineral reserves produce vast amounts of gold, silver, copper, nickel, and other minerals. Mineral exports earn billions of dollars for Australia, but mining often has devastating effects on the environment. Open-cut mining methods use massive machines to demolish whole mountains in order to get to the underlying minerals.

THE OZONE HOLE

Greenhouse gases such as carbon dioxide, methane, and nitrous oxide get trapped in the atmosphere and contribute to global warming. Changing weather patterns and rising sea levels are also linked to global warming.

In spite of its small population, Australia is a large producer of greenhouse gases. The country is responsible for about 2.1 percent of the world's total emissions. Most greenhouse gases produced by Australia come from the burning of fossil fuels such as coal, petroleum, and natural gas. Land clearing, which removes trees that absorb carbon dioxide, has also contributed to higher levels of greenhouse gases. In 2008 Australia signed the Kyoto Protocol to reduce greenhouse gases.

The wollemi pine tree is an endangered plant species.

Ozone-depleting substances also include chlorofluorocarbons, halons, carbon tetrachloride, methyl chloroform, methyl bromide, and hydrochlororfluorcarbons. These substances are used in air conditioners, refrigerators, fire extinguishers, aerosols, solvents, and agricultural fumigants. Excessive production and use of these substances has contributed to a general thinning of the ozone layer over most of the world, resulting in a hole in the ozone layer. This hole allows ultraviolet radiation to penetrate the Earth's atmosphere, causing serious health problems, such as an increased risk of skin cancer. Australia has the highest rate of skin cancer in the world. The government has made efforts to educate the public about the dangers of overexposure to the sun and the benefits of wearing hats and sunscreen lotions.

PROTECTING THE ENVIRONMENT

As the effects of land clearing and pollution have become evident, more Australians are playing an active role in protecting and sustaining their environment.

Spectators at a cricket Test Match apply free sunscreen provided by the organizers.

An abandoned uranium mine in Queensland. Leached minerals have caused the water at the mine to turn an unnatural shade of bright blue.

Uranium mining is a source of controversy in Australia not only because of damage to the environment but also because of the use of uranium in making atomic weapons. Australia's uranium is now sold only for electrical power generation, and Australia is party to the Nuclear Non-Proliferation Treaty as a nonnuclear weapons state. In 2010 to 2011 Australia produced more than 13,970,645 pounds (6,350,293 kg) of uranium oxide concentrate. It is the third-ranking producer in the world, behind Kazakhstan and Canada. Australia has 23 percent of the world's total uranium reserves. Protection of old-growth forests, or forests that have been kept intact since early European settlement, is an important issue. Logging companies are eager to exploit the large trees as timber. The wood-chipping industry, in which small pieces of wood are used to make paper and particleboard, is another source of concern. Conservationists argue that wood-chipping threatens wildlife habitats, causes soil erosion, and pollutes rivers.

The conservation movement in Australia remains strong. Many Australians support Greenpeace, the Wilderness Society, the Australian Conservation Foundation, and the Green Party.

MANAGING WASTE

The National Waste Policy, agreed to by all Australian environment ministers in 2009, is an efficient and environmentally responsible approach to waste management is Australia. The aims of the National Waste Policy are to avoid the generation of waste and minimize the amount of waste for disposal. Waste is to be managed as a resource and recycled. Waste recovery, treatment, and disposal are to be undertaken in a scientific, safe, and environmentally sound manner. Greenhouse gas emissions are to be reduced, energy conserved and produced, water used efficiently, and the productivity of the land to be managed. Educating people to discard their trash in a responsible way has met with some success, and local councils now provide recycling bins that are picked up by waste management authorities.

A garbage dump in Bicheno.

One day a year is set aside for a massive cleanup. On "Clean up Australia Day," people across the nation volunteer their time to remove litter from beaches, parks, and other public spaces. The first "Clean up Australia Day" was organized in 1989 in Sydney Harbour by Australian builder and yachtsman Ian Kiernan. The cleanup day movement has since been taken up by more than 120 countries.

Wind mills at a wind farm in the Atherton Tablelands.

ALTERNATIVE ENERGY SOURCES

Australia has significant wind and solar resources and limited large hydro resources. Hydropower is generated when water from a storage dam flows down through turbines. One drawback of such projects is that large tracts of land often need to be flooded to make an artificial dam. In the 1980s the damming of the Gordon River in Tasmania was stopped because of concerns by conservationists that native habitats would be destroyed. In 2007 to 2008 hydroelectricity was mainly generated in the eastern states, including Tasmania (57 percent of total electricity generation), New South Wales (21 percent), Victoria (13 percent), and Queensland (8 percent).

Making use of renewable energy plays a strong role in reducing Australia's greenhouse gas emissions and helping Australia stay on track to meet its Kyoto Protocol target. Already many Australian homes have solar-powered systems that heat water and generate electricity. These systems were a popular feature in the athletes' village at the 2000 Sydney Olympic Games, nicknamed the Green Games. Many telephone systems in remote areas of Australia are already powered by the sun. In 1999 scientists at the University of New South Wales were awarded a prize for developing the world's most efficient photovoltaic solar cell. These cells, which directly convert sunlight into electricity, are now commercially available worldwide. In July 2011 Australia's biggest solar power station was switched on in Alice Springs. The Uterne system features 3,000 solar panels and can generate enough power for about 300 houses.

Wind is a vast potential resource of renewable energy and wind farms can be found in Australia, particularly in the windy coastal areas. The wind turbines are tall structures, often more than 98 feet (30 m) high, and can generate significant amounts of electricity.

INTERNET LINKS

www.environment.gov.au/biodiversity/

This is an Australian government site detailing Australia's biodiversity conservation strategy.

www.environment.gov.au/biodiversity/publications/pubs/birds-08. pdf

This site features an Australian government PDF booklet with details on Australian birds. It also provides their status and the measures being taken to protect their habitat.

www.environment.gov.au/biodiversity/threatened/publications/ pubs/plants.pdf

This website contains an Australian government factsheet on threatened Australian plants.

www.nrm.gov.au/

This website is dedicated to "Caring for Our Country," covering topics from environmental stewardship to resource management.

AUSTRALIANS

An Australian girl dressed up for the Australian Football League finals at the Melbourne Cricket Ground.

6

LURED BY THE OPPORTUNITY FOR wealth and freedom in the "lucky country," people from all parts of the world come to Australia to start a new life. In 1945 Australia's population was approximately 7 million people and was mainly Anglo-Celtic.

Since then more than 6.5 million immigrants, including 675,000 refugees, have settled in the country. Today Australia has a population of more than 21 million people. Australia's indigenous population is estimated to be 483,000, or 2.3 percent of the total.

Australia is a product of a unique blend of new influences and established traditions. The Aboriginal and Torres Strait Islander peoples are the country's original inhabitants. They have been living in Australia for at least 40,000 years. The rest of the population are migrants or the descendants of migrants who arrived in Australia from about 200 countries since Great Britain established the first settlement at Sydney Cove in 1788.

A crowded street in the city of Melbourne.

trauma it caused. Sorry Day, an annual event that has taken place each May 26 since 1998, was set aside to acknowledge past laws and practices that brought suffering to Aboriginal people. During his more than 11 years as prime minister, John Howard refused to offer an official apology for past wrongs. Mr. Howard also refused to go to Canberra for the parliamentary apology in 2008 when Prime Minister Kevin Rudd delivered a national apology to the "Stolen Generation" on behalf of the federal parliament. The National Apology on February 13, 2008, was a momentous occasion.

The "Aborigine question" has polarized Australian society. Those who believe that the problems faced by the Aboriginal community were caused by unfair treatment by Europeans in the past include many members of recent governments. Of the many public programs and incentives instituted to help Aborigines, one in particular—giving land held sacred by the Aboriginal community back to the Aborigines—has been enormously controversial. Opponents of the so-called "land rights" legislation claim that Australia belongs to all Australians, not just to one particular section of the community. They also point to instances of mismanagement of land that has already been given to Aboriginal groups, including the subsequent selling of sacred land to mining companies.

Aborigines gathered outside Parliament House for former Australian prime minister Kevin Rudd's apology to the Stolen Generation.

A NEED FOR KNOWLEDGE AND IDENTITY

University lecturer and author James Wilson-Miller believes the current condition of the Aborigines would be greatly improved if they could raise their educational level and gain a sense of identity within their community. An Aborigine himself, Miller prefers to be known as a Koori, the Aboriginal word for the Aborigines from southeastern Australia.

Miller explains that he uses the term Koori because "it's my ancestral form of identification. Also, 19th-century thinking portrayed my people as simple, barbaric and savage, using the term 'aboriginal,' and we were not those things. I really can't identify with it because it doesn't give my people a separate identity."

INTERNET LINKS

www.abs.gov.au/websitedbs/D3310114.nsf/home/Home?opendocument

This website of the Australian Bureau of Statistics provides selected information and statistics on a wide variety of topics from economy to people, industry, and the environment.

www.antar.org.au

The ANTaR (Australians for Native Title and Reconciliation) website has information and links to issues and campaigns, media, and how to get involved in different events.

www.immi.gov.au/media/fact-sheets/08abolition.htm

This site contains a government factsheet about the history and abolition of the "white Australia" policy.

LIFESTYLE

Pedestrians in Sydney's busy city center.

7

" RELAXED AND FRIENDLY" IS THE Australian image made famous throughout the world by actor Paul Hogan, and to a large extent, this description holds true. Despite the pressures of modern society, Australians retain the old-fashioned values of hospitality, honesty, and modesty.

Many American students perceive Australia as being almost an extension of the United States. Because of Australians' close resemblance to

The diverse culture and lifestyle of Australia reflect its liberal democratic traditions and the cultural and social influences of the millions of migrants who have settled in the country since World War II.

A group of Australians enjoy a nice meal on a bright, clear day.

> ## LESSONS FROM THE SWAGMAN
>
> *During the depressions of the 1890s and 1930s, thousands of Australians, out of work and out of money, threw a few belongings in a bag, or swag; bid farewell to their families; and headed for the outback in search of work. From these men grew the tradition of the swagman. The swagman embodies many ideals that Australians greatly admire—ideals that influence Australian lives and attitudes. Here are a few of them:*
>
> - *"Mateship" refers to the bonds between close friends, or mates. These bonds are extraordinarily strong among Australians. Mates are expected to look after each other in times of need. Failure to do so—letting down a mate—is considered shameful.*
> - *"A fair go" refers to the belief that all individuals, regardless of birth or background, should be given an equal chance to succeed in whatever they choose to do.*
> - *The imagination of the Australian public is captured by stories of "battlers," or underdogs, who fight against overwhelming odds. But, although Australians are ever willing to help those in need, they also like to see individuals who flaunt their success be "brought down a peg or two." This is referred to as the "Tall Poppy Syndrome."*
> - *The "larrikin," or the rogue with a heart of gold, has a special place in Australian hearts. Famous larrikins range from actor and comedian Paul Hogan to Bob Hawke (prime minister of Australia in the 1980s and 1990s), and Ginger Meggs, a popular cartoon character.*

American culture, Australia has been considered a potential "51st state of the United States." This stemmed from the arrival of thousands of U.S. troops in the country during World War II. In addition to American influences on fashion, food, and entertainment, the Australian lifestyle has also been shaped by Europeans and, more recently, Asians.

THE FAMILY

Like people in other Western societies, Australians live in nuclear families made up of parents, brothers, and sisters. Because of the vastness of the continent and the willingness of the population to travel in search of work or a better lifestyle, contact between members of the extended family—grandparents, uncles, aunts, and cousins—can be infrequent. Family members do, however, get together for Christmas and Easter, often traveling thousands of miles across the country to share in the celebrations and catch up on family gossip.

From an early age, children are taught to be independent and self-sufficient. Although the law recognizes youths over the age of 18 as adults by giving them the right to vote, the 21st birthday is traditionally celebrated as the day of attaining adulthood. During the course of the celebrations (which can often be quite elaborate), the birthday boy or girl is sometimes presented with the symbolic "key to the door," meaning that they are now free to

A family having a barbecue in their backyard.

come and go from the family home as they choose, thus representing the beginning of an independent adult life. Festivities are usually accompanied by much drinking, embarrassing speeches, and elaborate pranks.

EDUCATION

All children between 6 and 15 years (16 in Tasmania) of age must attend school. After the first six or seven years of primary school, pupils progress to high school, where they spend a minimum of four years. Those intending to go to college or further advance their education spend an extra two years in high school in preparation for a public examination.

The school day starts between 8:30 and 9:30 A.M. and ends at 3:30 P.M., with breaks of half an hour for morning tea and an hour for lunch. Extracurricular activities such as sports and music or drama may keep children at school in the afternoons or on weekends. Education is free, unless parents decide to send their children to private schools. Annual fees at private schools range from under US$390 for institutions run by the Catholic Church to over US$25,000 at the nation's top independent schools.

Lessons come to life for these students studying wetland habitats.

THE SCHOOL OF THE AIR

Children in Australia's isolated outback who are unable to attend a regular school can instead enroll in the School of the Air (SOA). Until the 1950s children in remote areas would either have to go to a boarding school or complete their lessons by mail. In 1948 the Alice Springs RFDS (Royal Flying Doctor Service), which used pedal-powered radios for communication, was used to broadcast school lessons to children in the outback. Today the children use high-frequency (HF) radio receivers to receive their lessons. The HF radios allow the user to both send and receive messages, which means that students can now talk to each other as well as the teacher during classes. An SOA covers exactly the same curriculum as any other school in the state.

The Optus Interactive eLearning Initiative has brought the SOA into the digital age. Lessons can now be delivered via interactive two-way broadband satellite network. The network consists of a satellite hub in Sydney and five teaching studios in Alice Springs, Darwin, Broken Hill, Dubbo, and Port Macquarie. Satellite dishes and computers complete the network with 547 sites across New South Wales and the Northern Territory, including remote homesteads and properties, isolated schools, and indigenous settlements. Throughout the year, many students of the SOA rarely have the opportunity to meet their teachers or classmates in person because they may live as much as 497 miles (800 km) away. School camps are held annually to allow the students to participate in excursions with other students, both SOA and regular.

The clock tower of the University of Sydney, one of Australia's most prestigious universities.

Students who elect to further their education have a choice of going to a university, enrolling in a Vocational Education and Training course, or enrolling in Technical and Further Education at a technical college. The basic undergraduate course at most institutions is a bachelor's degree of three or four years' duration. Fields of study with the largest number of students in 2000 were business administration and economics (24 percent); arts, humanities, and social science (22 percent); and science (15 percent). Bachelor's degrees in other fields, such as medicine, engineering, or law, may take up to six years to obtain. In 2010 there were 3,510,875 students in Australian schools. Government and industry provide scholarships to help students of outstanding merit.

Australian education may be described as progressive. Instead of merely teaching the "three R's" (reading, 'riting, and 'rithmetic), pupils are encouraged to think, to question, and to argue the merits of existing beliefs. Emphasis is placed on the teaching of skills that will assist students in the adult world and encourage them to make a mature contribution to society. In recent years, there has been an increasing emphasis on information technology in schools. Children are learning computer skills at a very young age.

WORK

It used to be the case in most Australian families that the husband worked and the wife stayed at home to look after the house and children. However, changing attitudes and the rising cost of living have encouraged women to return to work. Today women make up more than half of the Australian public service workforce (57 percent), and this proportion is increasing. Two-thirds of all the Australian workforce is employed in the service industry, which includes the retail trade (1.29 million people), health, entertainment,

Australian social and community workers marching through the streets of Sydney to demand higher wages.

Australians are well known for their love for the sun, sea, and surf.

education, and finance. It also includes Australia's largest employer, the public service, which employed 163,778 staff in 2010.

In the past, long and hard battles were fought for the conditions enjoyed by workers today. Among the innovations now offered by most employers are flextime in which workers can choose the hours they work, a minimum wage in proportion to the work involved, and retirement programs to support workers when they stop working. In addition employers must observe strict antidiscrimination laws that prevent job applicants from being rejected on the basis of race, sex, age, or physical disability. Workers' rights are further protected by unions, which are strong and well organized.

AN ORDINARY DAY

Most Australians lead an urban lifestyle. From Monday to Friday the urban Aussie wakes up at around 7:00 A.M. After a breakfast of juice, cereal, toast, or eggs and bacon, family members go their various ways to start work or attend school.

The children attend school from about 9:00 A.M. to 3:30 P.M., and adults work from 9:00 A.M. to 5:00 P.M. The family gathers for dinner at about 6:30 P.M. After dinner the children do their homework and their parents might read or watch television. Most suburban families are in bed by 10:00 P.M. during the week.

THE GREAT AUSTRALIAN DREAM

The Great Australian Dream is the belief that owning a house is a measure of success and security. It is becoming more and more difficult to realize this dream as Australian property prices continue to rise. About 70 percent of houses are owned by their occupants, either with or without a mortgage. Approximately 30 percent of households rent their home. Urban housing is more expensive than rural, and Sydney's homes have the highest average value, followed by Perth, Canberra, and Brisbane.

The most common nonurban dwellings in Australia are freestanding one-floor houses built of brick or wood with a tiled or corrugated tin roof. Homes in warmer areas have open verandas that may run the length of the house. Many houses in the tropics are built on stilts. This traditional style of wooden dwelling is referred to as "Old Queenslander." In addition to allowing better circulation of air, this feature also protects the house from floods.

On the weekend, the Australian family may take part in some form of recreation, which can include a visit to the beach, a simple barbecue in the backyard with friends, or a drive to the countryside with a picnic or barbecue lunch. Being sports lovers, the Australian family may either pursue a favorite sport or watch it on television.

INTERNET LINKS

http://australia.gov.au/about-australia/australian-story/school-of-the-air

This website provides information on the history and development of the School of the Air and remote learning.

www.imagesaustralia.com/swagman.htm

This site introducing the Swagman also has the links to Australian poetry, songs, and images related to life in Australia.

RELIGION

The Uniting Church in Adelaide. Adelaide is also known as the City of Churches.

8

THE VARIOUS RELIGIOUS GROUPS in Australia are not confined to particular geographical regions. Because Australia is a secular state with no official state religion, followers of all religions are free to practice their faith under the full protection of the law.

Historically it has seldom been necessary to go to court to settle religious disputes, which tend to be few due to the easygoing nature of the Australian people.

The interior of Scots Presbyterian Church in Melbourne.

A group of Hare Krishna devotees chanting in the street of Melbourne's city center.

Since the Australian population is diverse, a wide variety of religions and places of worship is found throughout the country. Immigrants are encouraged to keep their own cultures, and different religious practices are viewed with tolerance, by both the government and the population.

Christianity is the major religion, but Judaism, Islam, and Buddhism also have many followers. In addition, religious sects—both Christian and non-Christian—also enjoy a following.

Although 64 percent of all Australians identify themselves as Christian, they do not all attend church regularly. The church nevertheless plays an important role in society, carrying out charity work and social programs.

THE CHRISTIAN CHURCHES

Also known as the Church of England, the Anglican Church of Australia was the first organized church to be established in Australia. It has played a dominant role in shaping the nation's legal, social, and political institutions.

Anglicans believe that religion cannot be separated from everyday life, and church leaders have a reputation for speaking out on social issues.

Australia's other major Christian religion, Roman Catholicism, was first introduced by Irish migrants in the early 19th century. More recent immigrants from Italy and Asia have strengthened the Church's numbers. Current figures indicate that 26 percent of Australians are Roman Catholic. Although this represents more than 5 million followers, the Roman Catholic Church has no Australian cardinal. Local policies of the Church are instead decided by a council of bishops.

Anglicans account for 20 percent of all Christians in Australia. The rest are mainly Presbyterians, Methodists, Lutherans, Baptists, and followers of the Eastern Orthodox Church. The Presbyterian Church is noted for its charity and missionary work—it runs the RFDS, which brings rapid medical attention to isolated families in the outback. The Uniting Church in Australia was formed in 1977 by a union of three churches: the Congregational Union of Australia, the Methodist Church of Australasia, and the Presbyterian Church of Australia.

The All Saints Anglican Church was built in Bodalla in 1881.

The exterior of the Great Synagogue in Sydney.

JUDAISM

Judaism has a long history in Australia. Jews were among the settlers who arrived in 1788 on the First Fleet from England. The community rapidly grew after World War II due to the influx of immigrants from the former Soviet Union and other parts of Europe. Many of these immigrants were victims of religious or political persecution in their home countries. The Jewish community in Australia consists of an estimated 88,800 people. Although most Australian Jews live in Sydney and Melbourne, synagogues can be found in over a dozen different cities across the nation.

BUDDHISM

Buddhism was introduced to Australia by Asian immigrants in the latter half of the 19th century. These immigrants included Chinese laborers who came to

The Fo Guang Shan Nan Tien temple in Wollongong.

In the 2006 Census of major religious affiliations 63.9 percent of Australians said they were Christians; 5.6 percent were from non-Christian religions; 18.7 percent said they had no religion; and 11.2 percent did not reply.

work in the goldfields, Japanese pearl fishermen, and Sri Lankans who settled in the northern part of Australia. The first Buddhist monastery, however, was only established 100 years later—in 1971, in the Blue Mountains region west of Sydney.

HINDUISM

Australia's Hindus are mostly immigrants from the Indian subcontinent, Southeast Asia, South Africa, and Fiji, who arrived in the country in the 1970s, after Australia abolished its "White Australia" policy. The criteria for granting immigration permits at this time became very strict. Therefore most of these immigrants were well-educated professionals. Although the Hindu community in Australia has a short history, the community has built several Hindu temples across the country. The first Hindu temple ever built in Australia, dedicated to the Hindu god Murugan, is located in Sydney.

ISLAM

Muslims praying in Lakemba Mosque.

Islam is one of the fastest-growing religions in Australia. It was introduced by Afghan camel drivers in the late 1800s. More than 360,000 people in Australia today identify themselves as Muslims. The religion is founded on the Five Pillars of Islam: the worship of Allah and the belief that Muhammad was the last prophet, daily prayers, fasting during the month of Ramadan, charity, and a pilgrimage to Mecca. Australian Islam is of a liberal brand, although devotees abide by the rules of their faith. Muslim law is not officially recognized by the Australian government.

INDIGENOUS BELIEFS

Australia's Aboriginal and Torres Strait Islander peoples follow their own spiritual beliefs and religion, which centers on a spirit world known as the Dreamtime or the Dreaming. They believe that this world existed long before the coming of human beings, and that it continues to exist parallel to ordinary life. The creation of the world by spirits and creatures from the Dreamtime is told in stories passed down from generation to generation. It is also described in Aboriginal art and dance.

The Dreaming has different meanings for different Aboriginal people. It is a complex network of knowledge, faith, and practices that derive from stories of creation, and which dominates all spiritual and physical aspects of Aboriginal life. The Dreaming sets out the structures of society, the rules for social behavior, and the ceremonies performed in order to maintain the life of the land.

THE SIKHS OF WOOLGOOLGA

Visitors to the coastal town of Woolgoolga will find it difficult to miss the domed white building overlooking the town. On closer inspection, they will see a notice instructing visitors to remove their shoes and cover their heads with a handkerchief before entering. This temple, known as the Guru Nanak Sikh Gurdwara (the Temple on the Hill), was built by the city's community of Sikhs, who make up about half of the town's population. Sikhs first settled in Woolgoolga in the 1940s to grow banana trees, and they now own about 90 percent of the local banana farms.

Guru Nanak founded Sikhism in India in the 16th century. Sikhism is a fusion of the tenets of Hinduism and Islam. Sikhs have adopted five objects (the five Ks) as a mark of their religion: uncut hair, breeches, a comb, a steel bangle, and a dagger.

The belief in one god is a basic tenet of Sikh scripture. Devout Sikhs express their worship in three ways: daily recitation of set passages of scripture, daily family worship, and regular worship at the temple.

Aboriginal belief can be described as a sophisticated form of animism. Groups have adopted local plants, animals, and features of the landscape as sacred totems, the most important being Uluru. Uluru is believed to be the spiritual center of Australia and the source of numerous spiritual forces permeating the country.

INTERNET LINKS

www.aboriginalculture.com.au/religion.shtml

This is a site devoted to Aboriginal religion, traditions, and ceremony. There are links to interesting old black-and-white photographs of Aboriginal bush foods, ceremonial decoration, fishing methods, and much more.

www.sikh.com.au/inaus/wool.html

This is an interesting website about the Sikh community in Woolgoolga.

A sign prohibiting alcohol in a public place in both English and the Aborigine language of the Martu in Western Australia.

A USTRALIAN ENGLISH IS RICH IN colorful slang and words borrowed from Aboriginal languages. Although the basic structure of Australian English is the same as that of the English in other English-speaking countries, Australian English contains subtleties that sometimes baffle non-Australians.

In its written form, Australian English follows mostly British style. The *Macquarie Dictionary* is the authoritative guide on standard Australian

A man reads one of Sydney's newspapers, *The Daily Telegraph.*

9

English is officially regarded as the national language of Australia. Apart from English and indigenous language, more than 160 other languages are also spoken in the home. Today's linguistic diversity stems primarily from immigration since 1945.

spelling and words. In recent years colloquial speech has been heavily influenced by American popular culture. Moreover the names of many of Australia's unique flora and fauna, its geographical features, and its towns are Aboriginal words. Early Australian pioneers were obviously hard-pressed to find names for their discoveries. Ernest Giles named a mountain range the Ophthalmia Range, after a disease that was plaguing him at the time!

CONVERSATION

The Australian accent, which is said to come from a mix of the London cockney and the Irish accent, characteristically pronounces pure vowel sounds as diphthongs (the union of two vowel sounds). The vowel sound is also sometimes changed entirely from the expected British or American pronunciation; so "day" becomes "dye" and "die" becomes "doi." The Australian accent can be heard to a greater or lesser extent throughout the country, and it gives Australian conversation a flavor of its own.

Young Australians gathering to watch Australia Day fireworks. Some English speakers find the Australian accent hard to understand.

Other English speakers have in the past not taken well to the Australian accent. Local filmmakers have had to dub or subtitle their work in response to complaints from foreign audiences. In 1911 one English author went so far as to say that "the common speech of the Commonwealth of Australia represents the most brutal maltreatment which has ever been inflicted on the mother tongue of the great English-speaking nations." Harsh words indeed!

THE AUSTRALIAN UNDERSTATEMENT

Making little of major happenings is a distinguishing feature of Australian conversation. Australians do not like to dramatize events, unless they are telling one of their "tall" stories. In this case, everything is blown out of proportion. However, understatement is the more usual feature.

Districts beset by torrential rains are "having a spot of bad weather." People in serious trouble are described as "having a bit of bother," and those who have achieved outstanding success have "done all right."

Schoolchildren in class. English is the language of instruction in Australia.

AUSTRALIAN SLANG

Much of Australia's colorful slang dates back to the country's early days. "Bludger," a criticism leveled at those who are lazy, owes its origins to the early colony's ruthless muggers, who struck their victims with heavy sticks (bludgeons) before making away with their possessions.

A CRASH COURSE IN AUSTRALIAN ENGLISH

Increasingly both spoken and written English in Australia follow American norms. Nevertheless several uniquely Australian words and expressions are still regularly used in everyday conversations. Here are some popular ones:

"She'll be right" means "It is under control, no need to worry." If something does not go well, you can refer to it as "a dingo's breakfast."

"G'day, mate" means "Hello, friend." The word mate *may be added at the end of a phrase or sentence, for example, "She'll be right, mate."*

Australians call Australia "Down Under" or "Oz." An Australian is an "Aussie." Within Australia, citizens from Queensland are known as banana benders, Victorians as Mexicans, Western Australians as sandgropers, and Tasmanians as Taswegians. Those who live in the country's extreme north come from the top end. The terms true blue *or* dinki di *describe someone or something that possesses genuinely Australian qualities.*

Footy means "football," which in Australia refers to games played under the Rugby League or Australian Rules codes of play. Australian Rules football is also known as Aussie Rules.

Local farmers are known as *cockies*, short for "cockatoo growers," since after spending a hard day sowing a field, a farmer would often wake up the next morning to find a flock of cockatoos, or Australian parrots, busily eating all his seeds. The farmer would "get his own back" by indulging in a meal of "bush mutton," or roast cockatoo! The galah, or rose-breasted cockatoo (*Cacatua roseicapilla*), has a reputation for being incredibly stupid. Thousands of galahs are killed each year because of their stubborn habit of pecking at live power lines. Silly people are good-naturedly referred to as "galahs."

Nicknames are an affectionate tradition in Australia. Usually friends' names are turned into nicknames by adding an "o" to the end of the first syllable. "David" becomes "Davo" and "John" becomes "Johnno." The "o" ending is also used for other things such as coffee breaks or smoke breaks, referred to as "smokos."

There has been a greater effort in Australia to preserve indigenous languages.

INDIGENOUS LANGUAGE

The Aboriginal and Torres Strait Islander peoples of Australia originally spoke between them about 250 languages consisting of as many as 700 dialects. These languages were separate languages, as distinct from one another as English is from Chinese. None of the Aboriginal languages had a written script.

Clashes with the first British settlers over land ownership, as well as the diseases brought by the new settlers, wiped out a number of indigenous groups and their languages. It is estimated that at least 50 were irretrievably lost in this way. In 2004 the National Indigenous Languages Survey found that only 145 indigenous languages were still spoken in Australia, and 110 of these were endangered. The survey found that only 18 languages were "strong" in the sense that they were spoken by all age groups. A census in 2006 found that 55,695 people, about one in eight indigenous Australians, said that an indigenous language was their primary language at home.

Indigenous languages are similar in sound and have a fairly common grammatical structure, but there are very few similarities in vocabulary. Still

To preserve Aboriginal languages, some indigenous communities have incorporated teaching Aboriginal languages into the curriculum.

there are some common words found in many of these languages, such as *jina* (jee-nah) for "foot," *mala* (maa-lah) for "hand," and *mayi* (mah-yee), meaning "vegetable."

Early European settlers recorded some words from the Darug, an Aboriginal group living in southeastern Australia. They included a number of words that have since been adopted into Australian English, such as *dingo*, now used as the name for a species of wild dog. For a long time, indigenous children attended schools taught in English. In the early 1970s bilingual education was introduced in some indigenous communities. Language centers have also been set up to keep alive the indigenous languages. Aborigines have also incorporated some English words into their language. Aboriginal Kriol is a language spoken throughout Australia that combines English and the indigenous languages.

NEWSPAPERS

Australians are avid newspaper readers. It is estimated that Australians buy about 4.5 million newspapers each day and about 3 million on Sunday. The Australian press is free to express its opinions with little censorship

Here are some common words and phrases used by the Australians:

Avago y'mug! *(Have a go, you mug!): A frustrated plea to people, or mugs, who are not trying hard enough. Used often at sporting events.*

Back of Bourke: *Australia's inland, or outback.*

Bloke: *A person, used in the same way as "guy" in the United States.*

Blowie: *A blowfly. Mosquitoes are referred to as "mozzies."*

Blue: *An argument.*

Bonza or beaut: *Good.*

Chook: *A chicken, as in "running round like a chook with its head cut off," a phrase used to describe people in a state of panic.*

Dobber: *An informant.*

Drongo or nong: *Idiot.*

Dunny: *Toilet.*

Fair crack of the whip: *A plea for leniency.*

Kangaroos in his top paddock: *Not of sound mind.*

Nipper: *A young child, also known as an ankle biter.*

Oz: *Australia. Australians call themselves "Aussies."*

Pom or Pommie: *An Englishman.*

Stone the crows: *An expression of surprise.*

Tinnie: *A beer can. Grog (alcohol) or plonk (wine) is drunk at pubs (bars).*

Yobbos: *Hooligans, also known as* hoons *and* ratbags.

from the government. Most newspapers have achieved a high standard of reporting, including the *Sydney Morning Herald* and Melbourne's *The Age*. Both newspapers were founded in the mid-19th century. *The Australian*, launched in 1964, is Australia's only national newspaper.

Newspapers with a large circulation, such as *The Daily Telegraph* from New South Wales, *The Age* from Victoria, and *The Courier Mail* from Queensland, are distributed throughout Australia. Each state capital has at least one morning and one afternoon newspaper.

The Australian Financial Review also has a national readership. Australia has several foreign language newspapers, with the largest circulation in Sydney and Melbourne. Greek and Italian migrants have the largest number of newspapers published in their native languages.

There are also several periodicals popular with all Australians. *Australian Women's Weekly*, a monthly magazine founded in 1933, has a wide readership among Australian women. There are another 150 publications in almost 40 languages. *The Bulletin*, founded in 1880, ceased publication in 2008.

Magazines on sale.

The office of television station Seven.

RADIO AND TELEVISION

Broadcasting and television are shared between the government-sponsored Australian Broadcasting Corporation (ABC) and a number of commercial stations. In the mid 1970s a special service was introduced to provide programs in foreign languages for the benefit of Australia's ethnic communities. It is operated by the Special Broadcasting Service (SBS) and funded by the federal government.

INTERNET LINKS

www.creativespirits.info/aboriginalculture/language/

This website provides detailed information on the language and culture of the Aboriginal and Torres Strait Islander people.

www.koalanet.com.au/australian-slang.html

This site includes a list of Australian slang words and their meaning.

ARTS

An artist paints a barramundi at the Injalak Arts and Crafts center in Australia's Northern Territory.

10

THE EARLIEST EXAMPLES OF visual art in Australia date back tens of thousands of years. Created by Aboriginal artists, these sculptures and cave paintings illustrate a mythical age when spirits and fantastic beasts roamed the land.

This period, called the Dreamtime, is celebrated in Aboriginal ceremonies called corroborees, in which singers and dancers paint Dreamtime symbols on their bodies and musicians beat clap-sticks or play the didgeridoo, a long hollow pipe made from a tree log.

Australia's creative and arts industries have built a global reputation for talent, creativity, and innovation. It is estimated that 90 percent of Australians participate in Australia's arts and cultural life.

Cave paintings by Aborigines give people a glimpse into what life was like thousands of years before the British arrived in Australia.

DESCRIBING THE LANDSCAPE

Australia's numerous art galleries are favorite attractions for both local and overseas visitors. They exhibit a diverse collection of both local and international art, including a number of works that have won the nation's most prestigious award—the Archibald Prize.

Painting the unique Australian landscape presented a major challenge to early European artists, who soon discarded the styles and rules they had learned in their homelands.

Rejecting the guidelines that were established by painters in the past, these artists, including Arthur Streeton and Tom Roberts, painted scenes *ën plein air* (in the open air) of Australia, particularly in Melbourne and the surrounding area. Over the years they were joined by other artists such as Walter Withers, Jane Sutherland, and Charles Conder. The Heidelberg School refers to this group of painters and the body of work they produced. Their work depicts people, places, and landscapes using impressionist techniques.

Artist Sir Sidney Nolan taking a break from working on his painting in 1955.

A DREAMTIME STORY: WHY THE STARS TWINKLE

One night, a long time ago, some women went out to dig for yams. They dug and dug with their digging sticks. Some were lucky and found lots of yams. Others did not find any. After returning to camp, those who had yams cooked them over a fire.

The women who did not find any yams felt ashamed. They decided to live in the sky so that people all around the world could see them. But as they were rising up to the sky, the women who were eating their yams rushed to join them and went up, too.

All the women turned into stars. On a clear night you can see them. The stars of those who did not find any yams are still and dim. But the lucky ones, the ones who found yams, twinkle as they eat their yams.

—from the Maung group of the Northern Territory

The lessons learned by these Australian impressionists influenced later artists, such as Norman Lindsay, Russell Drysdale, Fred Williams, and Sir Sidney Nolan.

The *Ned Kelly Series*, painted by Sir Sidney Nolan, has become as famous as Tom Roberts's *Shearing the Rams*. Nolan's works, along with those of a growing number of modern Australian artists, are becoming increasingly admired overseas. Pro Hart, a former miner, began painting full-time in 1958. His paintings of the Australian bush have won international acclaim.

A SCULPTURE THAT SINGS

The largest urban sculpture in Australia is 597 feet (182 m) wide and 221 feet (67 m) high. Its construction required 150 tons (136 metric tons) of concrete, 66,413 square feet (6,170 square m) of glass, 84 miles (135 km) of high-tension steel cable, and 1,056,000 tiles. It took nearly 20 years to build and cost $105 million. Within the 10 huge concrete shells that soar from its base are more than 900 rooms, including a concert hall that seats nearly 3,000 people, an opera theater, a library, and two restaurants.

The sculpture is in fact a building—the Sydney Opera House. It was conceived in 1955, when the New South Wales state government issued a challenge to the world's best architects to design an opera house fit for its capital city, Sydney.

Jørn Utzon, a Danish architect, won the competition. His vision of huge concrete shells soaring above the harbor like the white sails of a giant sailing ship captured the imagination of both the judges and the public.

On October 20, 1973, 16 years after the construction began, the Sydney Opera House was opened by Queen Elizabeth II. Since then it has hosted hundreds of concerts, operas, plays, exhibitions, and conferences each year. Visitors to the Opera House all agree that it possesses a unique and timeless beauty. It is, in the words of its designer, "a sculpture . . . a living thing." The Sydney Opera House was inscribed on the UNESCO World Heritage list in 2007.

LITERATURE

The outback and the exploits of its inhabitants have always been a favorite subject of Australian writers and poets. Henry Lawson wrote a number of

The iconic Sydney Opera House was completed in 1973.

well-loved bush stories, including "The Loaded Dog," a tongue-in-cheek tale of a faithful retriever that—much to its owner's horror—tries to return to him a stick of dynamite with the fuse still burning! One of Australia's most famous poems, "The Man From Snowy River," was written by Andrew Barton (Banjo) Patterson. The poem spawned the films *The Man from Snowy River* and *Return to Snowy River*, as well as the TV series *Snowy River: The MacGregor Saga*.

Prize-winning Australian author Peter Carey.

Contemporary playwrights and authors have focused more on the attitudes and beliefs of Australians. In *The Tree of Man* (1955), Nobel Prize—winning novelist Patrick White (1912—90) ridiculed many of the qualities that Australians admire about themselves. The book sparked long and heated arguments among Australians.

Born in 1943, Victoria native Peter Carey has won the Booker Prize, an award given annually to British Commonwealth authors, twice. His book *Oscar and Lucinda* won in 1988, and *True History of the Kelly Gang* won in 2001.

Immigrants have also contributed to Australian literature. In 1999 the Malaysian born Hsu-Ming Teo won the Australian Vogel Literary Award for her first novel, *Love and Vertigo*.

The country also has a long tradition of children's literature. Prominent children's writers include Ivan Southall, Patricia Wrightson, Colin Thiele, and May Gibbs.

MUSIC

Australian musicians perform a wide range of musical genres, including traditional classical, pop, country, jazz, rock, opera, alternative, and indigenous. The sound is uniquely Australian, influenced by the rhythmic

Peter Sculthorpe and Nigel Westlake. John Williams plays a guitar made by the renowned Australian luthier, Greg Smallman.

Other famous Australian musicians include Tony Emmanuel, Dame Joan Sutherland, Olivia Newton-John, John Farnham, Kylie Minogue, and Jason Donovan. Australian rock groups include INXS, Men at Work, and Midnight Oil.

FILMS

Australia holds the distinction of creating the world's first full-length silent feature film, *Soldiers of the Cross*, in 1900.

Going to the movies is a very popular pastime with Australians. Theaters come in all shapes and sizes, ranging from the city complex seating hundreds in air-conditioned comfort to the makeshift theater in the local town hall. Even small towns can have a modern theater; Esperance in Western Australia has a three-screen cinema complex and a population of fewer than 10,000 people.

The Australian film industry experienced a revival with the release of *Crocodile Dundee* (1986) and its sequel, which earned its producer and star, Paul Hogan, millions of dollars overseas. The movie grossed top dollar among local audiences, who enjoyed the stereotypical portrayal of Australia. Hogan originally worked as a rigger on the Sydney Harbour Bridge.

The *Mad Max* series starring Mel Gibson was a box-office hit. Other Australian films that have achieved cult status in recent years include *The Adventures of Priscilla: Queen of the Desert* (1994), *Strictly Ballroom* (1992), *Babe* (1995), *Moulin Rouge* (2001), *Australia* (2008), and *Red Dog* (2011).

Australian actors such as Mel Gibson, Nicole Kidman, Judy Davis, Cate Blanchett, and Hugh Jackman, and directors Peter Weir and Mark Anthony (Baz) Luhrmann have achieved a huge international following.

Australian film director Baz Luhrmann is responsible for some of the most popular films at the box office.

JUST DESSERTS

Australian audiences are well known for their appreciation of performing artists. One artist in particular, the prima ballerina Anna Pavlova, captured the hearts of the public during her tour of Australia in the 1930s. In tribute to the brilliant dancer, a local chef created a dessert consisting of a shell of meringue filled with whipped cream and fruit. The "pavlova," as it became known, was an instant success and soon became a national dish. Chefs have also created desserts for two world-famous Australian sopranos. The Peach Melba is named for Dame Nellie Melba (1861—1931), and La Stupenda Bavarois is named for Dame Joan Sutherland (1926—2010).

INTERNET LINKS

http://whc.unesco.org/en/list/166

This UNESCO World Heritage website provides detailed information on the Sydney Opera House.

www.artistwd.com/joyzine/australia/dreaming/index.php

This site includes a collection of creation stories from Aboriginal Dreamtime.

www.gurrumul.com/

This site is dedicated to Geoffrey Gurrumul Yunupingu, the hugely talented blind musician from Arnhemland. The site includes links to his lyrics and his music.

www.ironoutlaw.com/html/gallery.html

This website provides information on the artist Sidney Nolan and especially his *Ned Kelly Series* of paintings.

LEISURE

Amusement park-goers on a ride at the Sydney Royal Show.

11

AUSTRALIANS SPEND MUCH OF their free time outdoors, enjoying the country's wide-open spaces and pleasant weather. On weekends and holidays, people can be seen walking in the bush, relaxing at the beach, or simply outdoors, enjoying the sunshine.

OUTDOOR LIVING

Australia's 56 million acres (23 million ha) of protected forests are frequented by bushwalkers, hikers, campers, and fishermen. Fly

A hiker heading toward Mount Arapiles in Mount Arapiles-Tooan State Park in Victoria.

Australians enjoy their social and recreational pursuits and like to spend their leisure time with the family. Walking is the most widespread and popular form of exercise for almost 25 percent of Australians, whereas going to the cinema is the most popular cultural activity for those 15 years old or over. Being online at home is also a very popular leisure pursuit, with 72 percent of homes having Internet access.

fishermen troll streams in search of elusive brown trout and rainbow trout. Those after larger catches try their hand at offshore fishing, aiming to hook shark, marlin, or tuna.

Parks and plazas are common locations for open-air rock concerts, plays, and community celebrations. Moreover restaurants and hotels have outdoor areas for guests who wish to relax in the night air.

VACATIONS

Australians are great travelers, in their own country and overseas. Living or working overseas for a couple of years is virtually considered part of growing up. The most popular destinations for Australians going abroad are Europe and Great Britain. In addition many also travel to the cheaper and more accessible Asian countries and islands in the Pacific.

BEACH CULTURE

Australia boasts some of the best beaches in the world, with warm golden sand and cool turquoise water. Many of them are located in or within a

A surfing class in progress. Surfing is an activity enjoyed by many Australians.

reasonable distance from the capital cities. Sydney's Bondi (pronounced "bohn-dye") Beach is just 20 minutes from the city center. As the closest surfing beach to town, it attracts surfboarders as soon as the first rays of sunlight appear. Surfer's Paradise—on Queensland's heavily developed Gold Coast—is another popular spot for local residents and tourists. The islands on the Great Barrier Reef and several others off central and northern Queensland are excellent for beach vacations and for exploring the reef, either by glass bottom boat, snorkeling, or scuba-diving.

CRICKET

Cricket, Australia's most popular sport, is played by millions of sportsmen each season in their backyards, open fields, and sporting ovals (flat stretches of land used for sports). Cricket is played by two teams of 11 players, each taking turns to bat and bowl.

The fielding side's pitcher, known as the bowler, hurls a small ball at a "wicket" located at the opposite end of a 22-yard (20-m) grassy lane called

The Australian national cricket team poses with the Trans Tasman trophy in 2011.

the pitch. A batsman, or striker, from the opposing team stands in front of the wicket. Another batsman, or nonstriker, stands at the other end of the pitch. The bowler's aim is to hit the wicket with the ball. The batsman's aim is to prevent this by hitting the ball. A successful hit leads to the opportunity of scoring runs, which involves the batsman and his partner (the nonstriker) running to opposite ends of the pitch.

There are 10 different ways in which a striker can be dismissed. One way is when the bowler hits and breaks the wicket. The side that scores the most runs before all players are dismissed, or "bowled out," wins.

CRICKET TEST MATCHES The international form of cricket is known as a Test Match and is played over five days, with each side getting the opportunity to bat twice. Even then the match may end in a draw. A recent variation of the Test Match, the one-day match, is a shorter but more dynamic form of the game. It is often played at night under spotlights. Both Test Matches and one-day games attract huge, enthusiastic crowds, who turn out each

Australia playing a Test Match against New Zealand.

Regarded at the peak of his career as the perfect Australian, Sir Donald Bradman died in 2001 at the age of 93. Known simply as the Don, the country's greatest sports hero first brought his uncanny talent with the cricket bat to national attention as a young boy when he scored a century (more than 100 runs) in an interstate match in the 1920/21 season. The young Don was playing for Bowral School against Mittagong School. After being included in the national team, the Don went on to score numerous centuries, double centuries, and triple centuries—scoring a total of 50,731 runs and breaking countless long-standing records along the way. Under his captainship in the 1930s and 1940s, the Australian cricket team was invincible. Bradman himself retired in 1948 with a Test-batting average of 99.94 runs, a record that has never since been matched. He was knighted in 1949.

The Don was also at the center of a bitter dispute that soured relations between Australia and England. In a desperate effort to defeat the world's greatest batsman, the captain of the English cricket team that toured Australia at the end of 1933 resorted to unusual and highly dangerous tactics. Using the tactics known as bodyline, the English bowlers were instructed to bowl their balls not at the wickets, but at the batsman's body instead. Although bodyline tactics proved to be immediately successful even against the Don, the terrible injuries suffered by the Australian batsmen caused widespread public outrage against England. Cricket, a game steeped in the venerable traditions of sportsmanship and fair play, had become a bitter war. England won the Test series, but English cricket lost the respect and admiration of the Australian people. Bodyline tactics were declared illegal the following year.

summer to follow the fortunes of national cricketers against teams from England, India, New Zealand, Pakistan, South Africa, Sri Lanka, and the West Indies. The regular Test Matches between Australia and England are of special significance, since both teams fight for The Ashes, an urn containing the ashes of a wicket symbolizing the death of England's previous dominance of cricket in 1882. Australia's women's cricket team has also made a mark in the sport by winning the World Cup in 1978, 1982, 1988, 1997, and 2005.

SUMMER SPORTS

TENNIS   Cricket is undoubtedly the most popular spectator sport in Australia. However, more than a million Australians play tennis, maintaining a sporting dominance that has produced a number of international tennis superstars, including Grand Slam winner and two-time Wimbledon champion Rod Laver; Wimbledon champions Pat Cash, Evonne Goolagong Cawley, and John Newcombe; and U.S. Open champions Patrick Rafter and Lleyton Hewitt. Australia's national tennis teams have won the Davis Cup 20 times since 1950. The Australian Open, held in the state of Victoria, is one of the four Grand Slam events of international tennis and attracts the world's top players.

GOLF   Although golf is played all year-round in Australia, the major tournaments are held only during the summer. Australia is a favorite destination for avid overseas golfers who come on special golfing vacations. There are numerous clubs with world standard courses that are uncrowded and charge modest fees. Four-figure annual membership fees, common in the United States and Japan, are rare in Australia, even at the country's most exclusive golf courses. Australia's current top golfers are Adam Scott and Jason Day, ranked 24th and 38th in the world, respectively. In 1999 Karrie Webb won the U.S. Golf Titleholders Championship to become one of the world's leading female golfers. Each year Australia plays host to one of international golfing's major tournaments, the Australian Open.

SWIMMING   Australians are passionate about swimming. Many Australian homes have a pool of some sort in their backyard—from large swimming pools to small inflated ones. Public swimming pools are also very popular places to meet friends during the long summer months. Freestyle swimming, also known as the Australian crawl, was invented in Australia. In the 2008 Olympic Games the gold medal for the women's 4 x 100 m (328 feet) medley relay was won by Leisel Jones, Jessicah Schipper, Emily Seebohm, and Lisbeth Trickett. They set a new Olympic record and a new world record.

Australian Football League teams West Coast Eagles and Carlton Blues contest for the ball at a semifinals match. Australians are very passionate about Australian Rules football.

WINTER SPORTS

FOOTBALL   The sports calendar in the winter months is dominated by Australia's three varieties of football: Rugby Union, Rugby League, and Australian Rules. All three variations of football can be likened to a less structured and more free-flowing version of American gridiron football. Unlike American players, Australian players do not wear any protective clothing and must rely on their fitness, wits, and an element of luck to escape serious injury during the season.

The oldest variety, Rugby Union, used to be played on an amateur basis; it has since become a professional sport with international matches organized by the International Rugby Union. Australia is one of the world's top-ranking teams in Rugby Union, and became the world champion in 1991 by beating England and again in 1999 by beating France in the World Cup final. Rugby League, which closely resembles Union, has a strong following in the states of Queensland and New South Wales. Players sometimes switch from Rugby Union to Rugby League.

By far the most popular variety is Australian Rules (also called Aussie Rules or simply "footy")—a national sport that originated in the state of Victoria. Similar to Gaelic football, it is played on an enormous oval field. Games are hard and fast, with the action shifting from one end of the field to the other in the space of seconds. Australian Rules matches can draw huge crowds of enthusiastic fans. About 2.8 million Australians attended an Australian Rules football game during 2009 and 2010, according to figures released by the Australian Bureau of Statistics.

Australia's increasing concern over the safety of the football codes, as well as the growing immigrant population from southern Europe, has resulted in soccer's emergence as one of the country's largest participant sports. In addition to school and club teams, Australia has a national soccer team, the Socceroos. The high point in Australian soccer came in 1974 when the Australian national team qualified for the World Cup finals in Germany. Competitive soccer is played at club level, and Australia has had a National Soccer League since 1977.

NETBALL Australia's most popular women's sport, netball, was introduced to the country by the English in the early 1900s. The sport was first introduced as "women's basketball," and it is similar to that sport. In recent years men have started joining netball teams, and the number of men netball players is increasing each year. The Australian women's netball team has been a consistent winner of the World Netball championships, and it won again in 2011.

HAVING A PUNT

At 3:00 P.M. Australian Eastern Standard Time on the first Tuesday in November each year, workers put down their tools and supervisors interrupt inspections. Across the country, eyes and ears are glued to radios and television sets to witness the running of the premier event in the national horse-racing calendar—the Melbourne Cup. Although many Australians indulge in a bet, or punt, on the outcome of the 1.98-mile (3.2-km) event, Cup winners are very hard to pick, and luck plays as much a hand as knowledge. This race has become an international thoroughbred classic, and no other has such a strong hold on the Australian public.

Australians are avid race-goers, and meets are held all over the country at large city courses, such as Flemington and Randwick, and at numerous local courses in smaller towns. In addition to horse racing, Australians turn out to watch harness racing and greyhound races.

The Australian love of racing also extends to motor vehicles. The annual Bathurst 1,000 is an endurance race dominated by locally made cars. From 1985 to 1995 Adelaide, the state capital of South Australia, was the scene of the final race in the international Formula One Grand Prix competition. The Grand Prix has since been moved to Melbourne, where it is held in March. Like the famous Monaco circuit, the Melbourne Grand Prix is held in the city's streets. Famous Australian Formula One world champions include Jack Brabham, Alan Jones, and Mark Webber.

Camel races are also held in Australia. The Boulia Desert Sands camel races are the most popular in the country. Held every year in July in a small town in Queensland, these camel races attract a large crowd of locals and visitors.

INTERNET LINKS

http://australia.gov.au/about-australia/australian-story/melbourne-cup

This site provides detailed information on the Melbourne Cup, including details on the horses, the course, and the prizes.

www.bradman.com.au/home-bradman/

This website is dedicated to the famous cricket player Sir Donald Bradman.

FESTIVALS

A performer dressed as a giraffe at the Womandelaide Festival held in Adelaide.

12

AUSTRALIANS CELEBRATE EIGHT national holidays a year. In addition each state has its own holidays held at various times of the year. The two most important festivals in Australia are the two main feasts of the Christian calendar: Easter and Christmas.

CHRISTMAS

Christmas festivities begin more than a month in advance, in November, with schools and church groups staging Nativity plays celebrating

A Christmas street pageant in Adelaide.

There are many annual festivals held in Australia. Some are relatively small and community-based, such as the Thirroul Seaside and Arts Festival. The six-day Woodford Folk Festival is much bigger. Every capital city has an arts and cultural festival.

the birth of Christ. Evening gatherings are held in parks to sing Christmas carols by candlelight. On Christmas Eve churches around the country hold a midnight Mass. There are also special Christmas services on Christmas Day.

Christmas Day is celebrated at home with the family and close friends. The highlight of the day for many is Christmas lunch, an extravagant affair that requires many weeks of preparation. Some Australians still follow the British tradition of roast turkey followed by Christmas pudding, which is doused in brandy and set alight before being served. However, because Christmas falls in the middle of Australia's hot summer, many families prefer to hold a barbecue in the back garden or have a meal of cold meats or seafood and salads. The afternoon is the time for a nap or a lighthearted game of cricket with the children to recover from the elaborate lunch.

NATIONAL DAYS

AUSTRALIA DAY Also known as Foundation Day, Australia Day marks the anniversary of the arrival of the first British colonists (both free settlers and convicts) in Sydney Cove on January 26, 1788. The nation's birth is

The annual Tall Ships Regatta in Sydney Harbour is part of Australia Day celebrations.

celebrated on this day rather than on Federation Day, the anniversary of the creation of the Federation of Australia in 1901. This is partly due to the inopportune date chosen for federation—January 1—a day traditionally reserved to recover from the excesses of New Year's Eve! Australia Day is celebrated throughout the country in open-air festivals, as this holiday falls in the middle of the summer. People gather to watch reenactments of the first landing and to take part in contests that pay tribute to the nation's culture and history. At night fireworks light up the dusky skies high above the cities.

ANZAC DAY Every year on April 25, Australians observe a public holiday to mark ANZAC Day. This date is the anniversary of the start of Australia's most disastrous military battle—the Gallipoli campaign of World War I, in which ANZACs suffered horrendous casualties due to the poor leadership of their British commanders.

Military services are held at dawn on ANZAC Day at various war memorials. The service ends with the words "Lest we forget" —a reminder of

Australian servicemen taking part in the parade on **ANZAC Day**, which commemorates the memory and contributions of Australians who fought in the wars.

the horrors of war and the contribution of those Australians who braved it to defend their nation. The service is followed by a parade of servicemen from the various wars Australia has fought. The last Gallipoli campaign veteran, Tasmanian Alec Campbell, died in May 2002 at the age of 103.

THE QUEEN'S BIRTHDAY   Although her actual birthday is on April 21, the birthday of Queen Elizabeth II, queen of England and the head of the Commonwealth, is celebrated as a public holiday every year on the second Monday in June in all states except Western Australia, where it is celebrated on the Monday nearest September 30. The queen delivers a birthday speech on this day.

AGRICULTURAL SHOWS

The annual agricultural show has become a tradition of rural Australian life, although some shows take place in cities. The tradition was brought to Australia from Britain by the first settlers.

The agricultural show gives farmers the opportunity to show off their produce and catch up on the latest developments in agriculture. In addition

A cowboy competing at a rodeo at the Lismore Agricultural Show in New South Wales.

Clydesdale horses lined up for judging in the annual Royal Melbourne Agricultural Show.

to the judging of livestock and crops, awards are given for homemade arts and crafts, and a number of exhibitions are staged, including demonstrations by expert shearers (known as gun shearers) and cattle roundup competitions. These activities are accompanied by carnival rides and games. For people living in the bush, it is a wonderful opportunity to have some fun and meet new people.

Most agricultural shows are held in late summer or fall, and most towns host one show a year. The largest show held in Australia is Sydney's Royal Easter Show. Running for one whole week in early April, the show attracts millions of visitors each year. People come to examine samples of the best farming produce in the nation and enjoy the show jumping and rodeo events. Although rodeos are relatively new in Australia, several local riders figure among the top rodeo contestants in the United States.

AGQUIP More specialized agricultural shows include AgQuip, staged each year over three days in Gunnedah, New South Wales. Exhibitors display an astonishing variety of farming equipment, including pieces of state-of-the-art machinery that boast several-million-dollar price tags. The show attracts many overseas buyers looking for sophisticated and efficient methods to boost their crop production.

WINE FESTIVALS

Wine-producing areas host district festivals to promote their wines. These festivals, lasting up to several weeks, feature events such as outdoor picnics, wine-making demonstrations, and tours of vineyards. Free wine is also available for tasting, but enthusiastic visitors are warned to leave their cars at home or risk punishment under Australia's strict drunk-driving laws!

Barossa Valley Vintage Festival is held in South Australia's fertile Barossa Valley every April in odd-numbered years. The festival lasts one week and features more than a hundred different activities, including wine tasting, delicious food, arts and crafts, lively music, and stage performances.

Festival goers tasting some of Australia's domestic wines at a food and wine festival in Tasmania.

Adelaide's Bonython Hall illuminated as part of a northern lights event during the city's Festival of the Arts.

ARTS FESTIVALS

Arts festivals are held throughout the year in Australia's cities to encourage visits from overseas artists and to help develop local talent.

The Adelaide Festival of the Arts is held in even-numbered years. During this multi-arts festival, which was inaugurated in 1960, local and overseas artists, performers, and musicians flock to South Australia's capital to take part in plays, concerts, opera, theater, dance, the visual arts, master classes, outdoor entertainment, and exhibitions. The Adelaide Festival is also known for its high-profile events such as the Adelaide Writer's Week.

Similar festivals are held in Melbourne and Sydney each year. The Melbourne Festival, held in October, attracts world-class performers in the fields of theater, dance, music, opera, visual arts, and literature. Melbourne also hosts a popular comedy festival—the Melbourne International Comedy Festival—every year in April. Every January, the Sydney Festival opens with the unique Festival First Night, a feast of music, dance, and visual arts on

People take their beer drinking seriously in Darwin, in Australia's far north. In addition to being the chief city of the Northern Territory, the town is also known as the beer-drinking capital of the world since it is believed that Darwinians hold the distinction of consuming more beer per capita than residents of any other place in the world—60 gallons (230 l) a year! To keep up with the great demand, the town's breweries package their ales in the world's largest beer bottle—the half-gallon "Darwin stubbie."

Many of the drinkers in Darwin are in fact gathering the raw materials for a highly unusual race. Every August Darwinians gather to cheer on participants in the Beer Can Regatta, a charity race. Contestants take to the water in homemade boats, ranging from simple rafts to impressive model galleons, all made from thousands of empty aluminum beer cans. The race is the highlight of a day of festivities that, of course, includes much beer drinking.

The citizens of Alice Springs, in the Northern Territory's south, also hold an annual boat race, known as the Henley-on-Todd Regatta (a name derived from the British Henley-on-Thames Regatta) in late September. Undeterred by the fact that the Todd, the "river" on which the race is held, actually contains no water, the locals "sail" their bottomless boats by running on the sandy river bed. Later in the day, contestants return to the dry riverbed to stage mock sea battles between "pirates" and "Vikings" using high-pressure water cannons and bags of flour for ammunition.

the streets and in the parks of Sydney. This free event heralds the beginning of the three-week festival.

MUSIC FESTIVALS

Music festivals are also popular in Australia. Tamworth, New South Wales, hosts the Tamworth Country Music Festival. The festival was started in 1973 by a local radio station, 2TM. The ambition was to create a country music event that would support the country music awards they had staged.

The 10-day festival attracts more than 50,000 visitors. Australian country musicians, who enjoy a large following, compete for the coveted "golden guitar" awards given in recognition of excellence. A giant scale model of the award stands on the town's outskirts, welcoming visitors to the city.

UNUSUAL FESTIVALS

Australians will use any excuse for a party, as evidenced by some of the more unusual festivals held in the country. These include the Darwin Lions Beer Can Regatta and the Lions Alice Springs Camel Cup, a camel race held in Australia's outback.

During the Gay and Lesbian Mardi Gras, held in Sydney in February each year, the city's homosexual community takes to the streets in outrageous costumes. They and their elaborate floats are cheered on by thousands of onlookers. To raise funds for this event the Mardi Gras organizers hold an all-night costume party known as the Sleaze Ball.

INTERNET LINKS

http://www.australiaday.com.au/studentresources/history.aspx

This website provides information on the origins of Australia Day and why it is celebrated annually on January 26. The site also lists links to different events in addition to kids' activities, puzzles, and games.

www.awm.gov.au/commemoration/anzac/

This website has detailed information about ANZAC Day, Remembrance Day, war history, museums, wreath laying, and customs.

www.barossavintagefestival.com.au/

This website contains a wealth of information on the biannual Barossa Vintage Festival.

FOOD

Fresh produce at a market in Adelaide.

13

T RADITIONALLY AUSTRALIA IS A country of meat eaters. Typical Australian fare consists of meat for the three main meals of the day, with a breakfast of grilled lamb chops, sausages, bacon, and eggs; cold meats for lunch; and a dinner of roast or grilled lamb, beef, or pork. Meals are served with cooked vegetables and are accompanied by bread.

The influence of new cuisines and increasing health consciousness has blunted the Australian appetite for meat, although in some families it

Most Australians enjoy a barbecue on the weekend.

Before white settlement the indigenous people of Australia survived off the native plants and animals that were available. Nowadays Australian food is influenced by the large number of immigrants from Mediterranean, Asian, and other countries. Culinary dishes reflect Australia's multicultural society.

Unlike their counterparts in the United States, Japan, and other countries, Australian diners prefer beef from pasture-raised cattle to beef from grain-fed cattle. Australians argue that cattle free to feed in pastures produce a more flavorful meat that is healthier because it contains less marbled fat.

Furthermore many locals believe that the methods used to raise grain-fed cattle are cruel since the animals are not allowed to walk freely in the pastures and exercise. They also argue that grain-feeding methods are wasteful since the grains used to feed the cattle could instead be made into products for human consumption.

remains the focus of most meals. Rising prices and the faster pace of modern life have also affected the traditional Sunday roast, a sumptuous lunch that takes many hours to prepare. Vegetarianism has become more popular in recent years, and most restaurants now offer vegetarian options on their menu.

FOOD FOR THE OUTDOORS

Camping in the Australian bush is not complete without damper and billy tea. Damper is a bread made from flour, salt, sugar, soda, and milk. The ingredients are combined and traditionally cooked in a cast-iron pot with a lid. The pot is covered with the hot coals of an open fire and cooked until a blackened crust forms. When eaten with generous portions of treacle, a thick syrup similar to molasses, damper is known as cocky's joy. The perfect drink to have with damper is billy tea. After water boils in a camp can, known as a billy, a few tea leaves and the odd gum tree leaf are thrown in for about a minute. The cook settles the tea leaves by tapping the billy with a stick, then grasps the handle firmly and swings the billy around in a wide circle several times to cool the tea. To avoid disaster, this last step should be left to those with experience!

FAST FOOD

Fast food, which caters to the Australian outdoor lifestyle, has grown in popularity in recent years.

Hamburgers, which were made popular by American soldiers stationed in Australia during World War II, have become a local culinary institution. Hamburgers sold at small neighborhood shops, known as corner shops, are huge, cramming a beef patty, bacon, a fried egg, cheese, onions, lettuce, tomatoes, beets, cucumber, and a slice of pineapple into a buttered bun.

Equally popular is the meat pie, a fist-sized fast food that can be eaten on the run. Originally brought from England by early settlers in the 1800s, meat pies are now viewed as Australia's national dish.

FAVORITE DISHES

Australian
meat pies.

Some foods have become so popular with Australians that they are regarded as culinary institutions, much like the hamburger.

PUMPKIN SCONES   A long domestic tradition in northern Australia, pumpkin scones enjoyed a recent revival at the hands of Lady Florence Bjelke-Petersen, wife of former federal senator Joh Bjelke-Petersen. She baked vast quantities of the little snacks to sustain her husband, then premier of Queensland, through the rigors of government. The scones obviously worked, since Joh Bjelke-Petersen enjoyed an unparalleled career in Australian politics, becoming by far the longest-serving state premier in the nation's history. He was also the most flamboyant and controversial premier in modern Australian politics.

LAMINGTONS These delicate little sponge cakes are particularly popular at festivals and shows. Made from flour, eggs, milk, sugar, butter, and

BUSH TUCKER

Unable to eke any sustenance from what they saw as the inhospitable bush, European settlers brought their crops and livestock with them. The ensuing clearing of the landscape to create pastureland resulted in environmental havoc. Today, in seeking more environmentally friendly solutions to the problem of sustaining a nation, interest is growing in the food or "bush tucker" that is provided naturally by the Australian environment, a resource that has been exploited by the Aborigines for thousands of years. Bush tucker includes dubious delicacies such as the Witchetty grub, a fat, white slug-like creature that inhabits the bush of the same name and is traditionally eaten raw. In recent years Witchetty grubs have been exported as "wood lobsters," with the recommendation to serve them lightly sautéd with a few herbs and spices.

Although the kangaroo formed a staple part of the Aboriginal diet, present-day Australians are generally less enthusiastic about eating the country's animal emblem. Nevertheless kangaroo steaks and stews and kangaroo tail soups are still eaten today, and the meat is available in many supermarkets. Kangaroo tail soup was in fact so popular in the 1960s that it was canned for export. The Australian kangaroo industry estimates that it exports kangaroo meat to more than 55 countries. Crocodile steaks are also eaten. There is an undoubted secret satisfaction in eating crocodile, since each year one or two unfortunate swimmers fall victim to these beasts.

If a crocodile or kangaroo is not handy, meals can be had from emus, wallabies, camels, snakes, turtles, birds, all kinds of fish and eels, ants, wild bees, wild grains and grasses, and native roots, fruit, and figs. A parasitic insect that attacks the mulga tree causes swollen lumps to appear on its branches. These are sweet and juicy inside and are referred to as "mulga apples." Plants and smaller animals are often eaten raw. Larger animals are usually roasted in hot coal.

In addition to its exotic appeal, bush tucker is nutritious and tasty. Those adventurous enough to give it a try can visit restaurants that specialize in this cuisine.

vanilla, the baked cake is sliced into 2-inch (5-cm) cubes that are then dipped in chocolate and covered with desiccated coconut. The lamington is also connected to Queensland politics. It is said to have been created by the wife of 19th-century Queensland Governor Baron Lamington, who served the cake bearing his name to his campaign workers.

Lamingtons are sweet, small sponge cakes.

PAVLOVA The pavlova, also known as the "pav," is a favorite dessert created in the early 1900s in honor of Russian ballerina Anna Pavlova by Western Australian chef Bert Sachse. The pavlova consists of a crisp, smooth shell of meringue, filled with whipped cream, ice cream, and fresh fruit.

ANZAC BISCUITS First made during World War I by Australian mothers for their boys who were fighting overseas, ANZAC biscuits are crisp and long-lasting. They have a pleasant gingery tang since they contain ginger, coconut, brown sugar, and golden syrup. ANZAC biscuits are also known for being extremely hard, and some may even double as a tent peg hammer or a heavy-duty paperweight!

VEGEMITE A thick, black yeast extract made in Australia by Kraft Foods, Vegemite is a longtime favorite sandwich filling and an ingredient in many spicy dishes. Vegemite sandwiches are best made using thick slices of freshly baked white bread. After generously buttering the slices, apply a small amount of Vegemite. Those unacquainted with its unique flavor should then proceed with caution, taking only modest bites and having a large drink on hand to wash it down. Vegemite is definitely an acquired taste, and its immense popularity among Australians is a frequent source of wonder to overseas visitors.

**Banana crops
in Nerada.**

VEGETABLES AND FRUITS

Vegetables that grow in abundance in Australia include sweet potatoes, eggplant, cucumbers, zucchini, lettuce, cabbage, beans, peas, asparagus, tomatoes, carrots, mushrooms, and onions. One of the most popular vegetables is pumpkin, which is used in all kinds of dishes.

Fruit is abundant and available all year-round, since many varieties can be grown in various parts of the country at different times of the year. These include apples, pears, mangoes, papayas, grapes, custard apples, nectarines, peaches, plums, and berries. Citrus crops of oranges, lemons, limes, and grapefruit are grown in all Australian states except Tasmania. The floods followed by Cyclone Yasi during 2010 and 2011 devastated the agriculture of New South Wales and Queensland and pushed up the price of many fruits and vegetables.

HONEY

The honeybee is not native to Australia. Honeybees were introduced in 1822 on board the ship *Isabella*, from England. The honeybees adapted so successfully that other species have since been imported from Italy, Yugoslavia, and North America. Australia has many floral sources that are unique to the country and ideal for making honey, so a wide range of colors and tastes are produced. The most popular honey flavors come from blue gum, karri, leatherwood, yellow box, and stringy bark trees. Honey is produced commercially for export. Organic honey is also produced by enthusiastic apiarists with a just a few hives on their land. Honey has been nicknamed Australia's liquid gold.

BYO

Many Australian restaurants are BYO—that is, you can "Bring Your Own" wine to enjoy with the meal. Some restaurants are also licensed to serve their own liquor, so the diner can choose the convenience of ordering from a wine list or the cheaper option of buying a bottle from the liquor store or supermarket. The waiter will open it and serve it to you just as if it had come from the wine list.

BYO restaurants are usually smaller and less expensive than premises licensed to sell liquor. They generally serve very good food. BYO places are most popular in Melbourne and Sydney.

INTERNET LINKS

www.aussiecooking.com.au

This site features many of Australia's typical recipes, including pumpkin soup and lamingtons. There is also a link to Australian native food recipes, which are recipes that use native foods, such as wattleseed and lemon myrtle.

www.honeybee.org.au

This is the Australian honeybee industry website that provides a link to the fascinating PDF file "The Wonderful Story of Australian Honey," which describes bees and honey production.

www.theepicentre.com/Australia/aufood2.html

This website has a list of bush tucker foods and links to detailed information on some edible native plant species.

ANZAC BISCUITS

These cookies are named after the Australian and New Zealand army troops that fought alongside the British in World War I. This recipe makes a dozen cookies.

Ingredients

2 cups (500 ml) rolled oats

$1/3$ cup (85 ml) shredded coconut

$1/2$ cup (125 ml) brown sugar

1 cup (250 ml) flour

$1/2$ cup (125 ml) plus 1 teaspoon (5 ml) melted butter

1 tablespoon (15 ml) golden syrup

2 tablespoons (30 ml) boiling water

1 teaspoon (5 ml) baking soda

1 tablespoon (15 ml) ground ginger

Combine oats, coconut, brown sugar, flour, and melted butter in a large bowl. Add golden syrup. Dissolve baking soda in boiling water and add to mix. Lastly add ground ginger to mix. Using a tablespoon, break the mix into 12 to 15 small balls and place on a greased cookie sheet. Place in oven and bake at 350°F (180°C) for 15 to 20 minutes, or until golden-brown and crispy.

AUSTRALIAN MEAT PIE

An Australian meat pie is a hand-sized meat pie containing largely diced or minced meat and gravy, sometimes with onion, mushrooms, or cheese and often consumed as a takeaway food snack. This recipe makes about 10 pie servings.

Ingredients

1 pound (500 g) ground beef

20 small mushrooms, sliced

2 tablespoons (30 ml) vegetable oil

Salt and pepper to taste

1 cup (250 ml) beef stock (or 1 beef bouillon cube dissolved in 1 cup (250 ml) boiling water)

1½ tablespoons (22.5 ml) flour

Ready-made puff pastry, thawed

1 egg yolk

Tomato sauce

In a frying pan, fry beef and mushrooms in oil over medium heat until browned. Add salt and pepper to taste. Add beef stock and flour and simmer until a thick gravy forms. Remove from heat and cool. Divide pastry into two portions and roll out two rounds ³/₄-inch (1.5-cm) thick. Line a greased 8-inch (20-cm) diameter pie plate. Leave some pastry for the top crust. Fill pie plate with beef mixture. Cover with pastry top and trim edges. Brush pastry top with egg yolk mixed with a little water. Bake in 425°F (220°C) oven until the top is brown (about 5 minutes), then at moderate heat of 350°F (180°C) for 10 minutes. Pour some tomato sauce on each slice and enjoy.

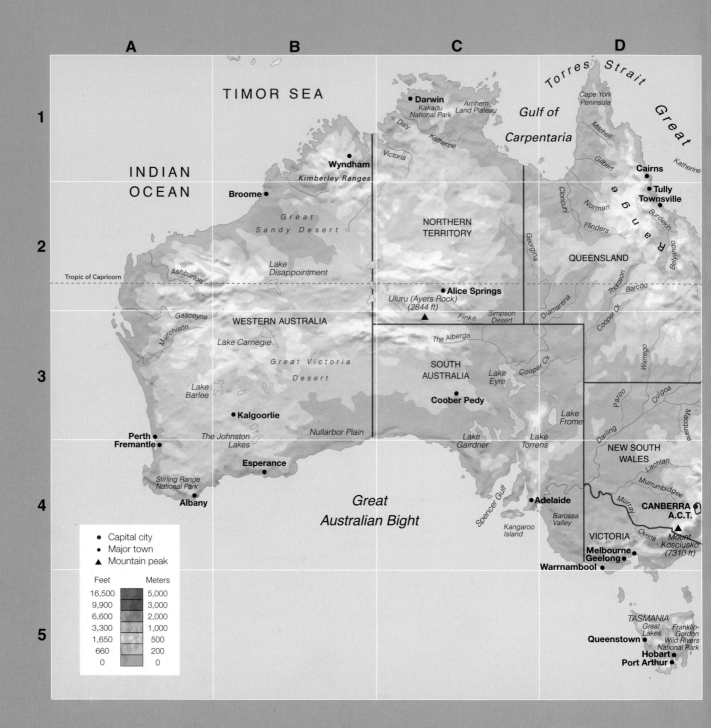

	A	B	C	D

1

2

3

4

5

TIMOR SEA

INDIAN
OCEAN

• Darwin
Kakadu
National Park

Arnhem
Land Plateau

Gulf of
Carpentaria

Torres Strait

Great

Cape York
Peninsula

Mitchell

• Cairns

• Tully
Townsville

• Wyndham

Kimberley Ranges

Daly

Victoria

Katherine

NORTHERN
TERRITORY

Georgina

Gilbert

Norman

Cloncurry

Flinders

Burdekin

Belyando

• Broome

Great
Sandy Desert

Lake
Disappointment

QUEENSLAND

Thomson

Barcoo

Tropic of Capricorn

Ashburton

• Alice Springs

Uluru (Ayers Rock)
(2844 ft)
▲

Simpson
Desert

Diamantina

Cooper Ck

Gascoyne

Murchison

WESTERN AUSTRALIA

Lake Carnegie

The Alberga

Finke

Warrego

SOUTH
AUSTRALIA

Lake
Eyre

Cooper Ck

Lake
Barlee

Great Victoria
Desert

Paroo

Culgoa

Macquarie

• Coober Pedy

Lake
Frome

Darling

NEW SOUTH
WALES

• Kalgoorlie

Lake
Torrens

Lachlan

Perth •
Fremantle •

The Johnston
Lakes

Nullarbor Plain

Lake
Gairdner

Murrumbidgee

Murray

CANBERRA
A.C.T.

• Esperance

Stirling Range
National Park

• Albany

Great
Australian Bight

Spencer Gulf

• Adelaide

Barossa
Valley

Kangaroo
Island

Ovens

VICTORIA

Melbourne •
Geelong •

Mount
Kosciusko
(7310 ft)
▲

Warrnambool •

• Capital city
• Major town
▲ Mountain peak

Feet		Meters
16,500		5,000
9,900		3,000
6,600		2,000
3,300		1,000
1,650		500
660		200
0		0

TASMANIA
Great
Lakes

Franklin-
Gordon
Wild Rivers
National Park

Queenstown •

Hobart •
Port Arthur •

MAP OF AUSTRALIA

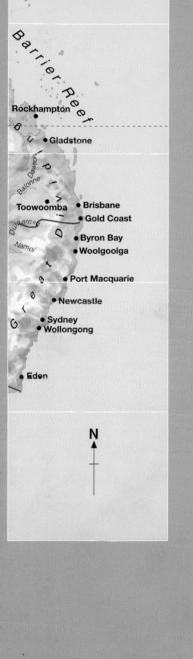

E

CORAL SEA

Barrier Reef

Rockhampton

Gladstone

Dawson
Balonne

Toowoomba • Brisbane
• Gold Coast
Dumaresq
Namoi • Byron Bay
• Woolgoolga

• Port Macquarie

• Newcastle
• Sydney
Wollongong

• Eden

N

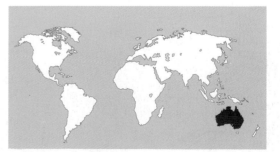

ECONOMIC AUSTRALIA

Natural Resources

Coal   Iron

Diamonds   Opals

Fish   Silver

Gas   Timber

Gold   Uranium

Hydroelectricity

Farming

Cattle

Fruit

Milk

Rice

Sheep

Sugar

Wheat

Manufacturing

Cotton

Tin

Wine

ABOUT THE ECONOMY

OVERVIEW

Australia's capitalist economy depends heavily on the export of agricultural products, minerals, metals, and fuels. Commodities account for 57 percent of total exports, so a decrease in world commodity prices can have a big impact on the country's economy. Floods and Cyclone Yasi in 2010 and 2011 resulted in the temporary closure of coal mines and the decimation of many crops, such as sugarcane and bananas. This has affected Australia's export earnings. The government is pushing for increased exports of manufactured goods, but competition in international markets continues to be severe. According to government statistics, Australia's two-way trade in services and goods was worth over $550 billion in 2010.

GROSS DOMESTIC PRODUCT (GDP)
US$882.4 billion (2010 estimate)

GDP PER CAPITA
$41,000 (2010 estimate)

GDP SECTORS (2010 estimate)
Agriculture: 3.9 percent
Industry: 25.6 percent
Services: 70.5 percent

CURRENCY
1 USD = 0.97 AUD (January 2012)

WORKFORCE
11.87 million (2010 estimate)

UNEMPLOYMENT RATE
5.2 percent (2010 estimate)

INDUSTRIES
Chemicals, food processing, manufacturing of industrial and transportation equipment, mining, steel

AGRICULTURAL PRODUCTS
Barley, fruits, sugarcane, wheat

ANIMAL PRODUCTS
Cattle, poultry, sheep

MAJOR EXPORTS
Aluminum, coal, gold, iron ore, machinery and transportation equipment, meat, wheat, wool

MAJOR IMPORTS
Computer and office machines, crude oil and petroleum products, machinery and transportation equipment, telecommunications equipment

MAJOR TRADING PARTNERS
ASEAN, China, Germany, United Kingdom, India, Hong Kong, Japan, New Zealand, South Korea, Thailand, Singapore, United States

TRANSPORTATION
Number of airports: 465 (2010)
Railways: 23,889 miles (38,445 km)
Roadways: 505,157 miles (812,972 km)

CULTURAL AUSTRALIA

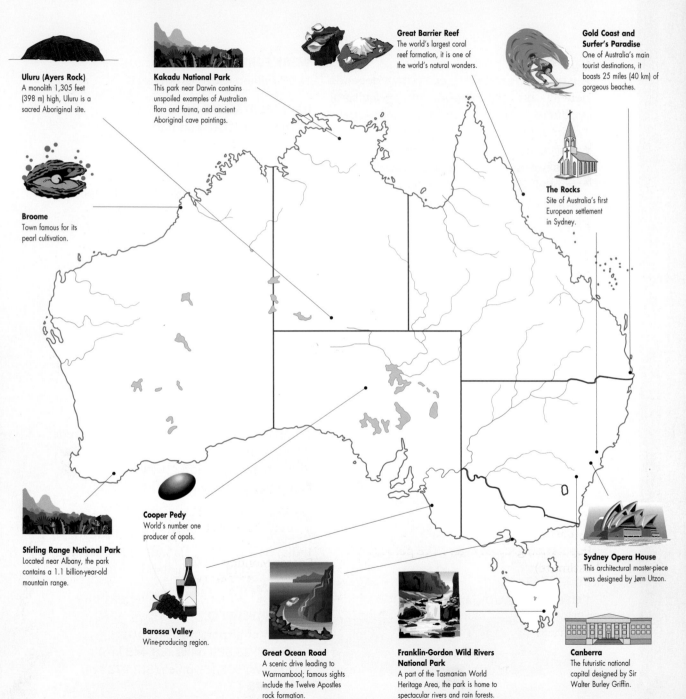

Uluru (Ayers Rock)
A monolith 1,305 feet (398 m) high, Uluru is a sacred Aboriginal site.

Broome
Town famous for its pearl cultivation.

Kakadu National Park
This park near Darwin contains unspoiled examples of Australian flora and fauna, and ancient Aboriginal cave paintings.

Great Barrier Reef
The world's largest coral reef formation, it is one of the world's natural wonders.

Gold Coast and Surfer's Paradise
One of Australia's main tourist destinations, it boasts 25 miles (40 km) of gorgeous beaches.

The Rocks
Site of Australia's first European settlement in Sydney.

Stirling Range National Park
Located near Albany, the park contains a 1.1 billion-year-old mountain range.

Cooper Pedy
World's number one producer of opals.

Barossa Valley
Wine-producing region.

Great Ocean Road
A scenic drive leading to Warrnambool; famous sights include the Twelve Apostles rock formation.

Franklin-Gordon Wild Rivers National Park
A part of the Tasmanian World Heritage Area, the park is home to spectacular rivers and rain forests.

Sydney Opera House
This architectural master-piece was designed by Jørn Utzon.

Canberra
The futuristic national capital designed by Sir Walter Burley Griffin.

ABOUT THE CULTURE

OFFICIAL NAME
Commonwealth of Australia

CAPITAL
Canberra

DESCRIPTION OF FLAG
Blue background with Southern Cross on right, Union Jack on top left corner, and single star on bottom left.

GOVERNMENT
Federation of states with a parliamentary government, with the British monarch as head of state.

NATIONAL ANTHEM
Advance Australia Fair

POPULATION
21,7611,711 (July 2011 estimate)
Population growth rate: 1.148 percent (2011 estimate)

AREA
Total: 2,988,902 square miles (7,741,220 square km)

ETHNIC GROUPS
Caucasian: 92 percent; Asian: 7 percent; Aboriginal and other: 1 percent

RELIGION
Catholic: 25.8 percent (2006 census); Anglican: 18.7 percent (2006 census); Uniting Church: 5.7 percent (2006 census); Presbyterian and Reformed: 3 percent (2006 census); Eastern Orthodox: 2.7 percent (2006 census); Other Christian: 7.9 percent (2006 census); Buddhist: 2.1 percent (2006 census); Muslim: 1.7 percent (2006 census); Other: 2.4 percent (2006 census); Unspecified: 11.3 percent (2006 census); None: 18.7 percent (2006 census)

LIFE EXPECTANCY
Male: 79.4 years (2011 estimate)
Female: 84.35 years (2011 estimate)

LITERACY RATE
Definition: age 15 and over can read and write
Over 99 percent (2011 estimate)

NATIONAL HOLIDAYS
January 1—New Year's Day
January 26—Australia Day
March/April—Good Friday, Vigil of Easter, Easter Monday
April 25—ANZAC Day
Early June—Queen Elizabeth's birthday
December 25—Christmas Day
December 26—Boxing Day

TIME LINE

IN AUSTRALIA	IN THE WORLD

A.D. 1500s–1600s
Portuguese and Dutch explorers visit Australia.

1206–1368
Genghis Khan unifies the Mongols and starts conquest of the world. At its height, the Mongol Empire under Kublai Khan stretches from China to Persia and parts of Europe and Russia.

1770
Captain James Cook maps the eastern coast of Australia and claims it for England.

1776
U.S. Declaration of Independence

1788
First European settlers arrive in Botany Bay on First Fleet from England.

1789–99
The French Revolution

1829
Western Australia is founded as an English colony.

1850s
Discovery of gold in New South Wales and Victoria leads to "gold rush."

1894
Women gain the right to vote in South Australia.

1901
States unite under the Commonwealth of Australia on January 1.

1911
Canberra is founded and designated as the capital.

1914
World War I begins.

1915
Heroic ANZAC campaign against Turks in Gallipoli during World War I

1939
Australia enters World War II.

1939
World War II begins.

1945
The United States drops atomic bombs on Hiroshima and Nagasaki. World War II ends.

1956
Melbourne hosts Olympic Games.

1975
Labor government is dismissed by governor-general.

1992
The High Court's Mabo decision extends Aboriginal land and customary rights.

IN AUSTRALIA	IN THE WORLD
	1997
2000	Hong Kong is returned to China.
Sydney hosts Olympic Games.	**2001**
2002	Terrorists crash planes into New York,
A bomb outside a nightclub in Bali, Indonesia, kills 88 Australian citizens.	Washington D.C., and Pennsylvania.
2003	**2003**
Bushfires destroy more than 500 homes in Canberra, and other fires rage in New South Wales, Victoria, and Tasmania.	War in Iraq begins.
2004	**2004**
Bomb attack outside Australian Embassy in Jakarta, Indonesia, kills at least nine people.	Eleven Asia countries are hit by giant tsunami, killing at least 225,000 people.
	2005
2007	Hurricane Katrina devastates the Gulf Coast of the United States.
Kevin Rudd leads the opposition Labor Party into power. He signs documents ratifying the Kyoto Protocol on climate change, reversing the previous government's policy.	
2008	**2008**
Government makes a public apology for past wrongs committed against the indigenous population.	Earthquake in Sichuan, China, kills 67,000 people.
2009	**2009**
Bushfires in the state of Victoria leave around 180 people dead.	Outbreak of flu virus H1N1 around the world
2010	
Julia Gillard becomes prime minister. Queensland is hit by floods that kill 22 people and are described as the most expensive natural disaster in the country's history.	
2011	**2011**
Cyclone Yasi makes landfall in Queensland, causing extensive damage to property and crops.	Twin earthquake and tsunami disasters strike northeast Japan, leaving more than 14,000 dead and thousands more missing.

GLOSSARY

Aborigines
Earliest inhabitants of Australia.

artesian wells
Wells located under a layer of impermeable rock in which water rises continuously under pressure.

billabong
A sheltered waterhole.

billy
A cylindrical container with a close-fitting lid.

bush
Countryside.

colloquial speech
Speech used in informal conversation.

corroborees
Sacred Aboriginal ceremonies in which dancers paint Dreamtime symbols on their bodies.

didgeridoo
An Aboriginal wind instrument consisting of a hollow pipe made from a tree log.

jumbuck
Sheep.

Koori
Word used by Aborigines to describe themselves.

matilda
Bed roll, usually carried by swagmen.

nipper
A young child.

outback
Remote, sparsely populated Australian country region.

over
The six throws taken by a bowler in a cricket Test Match before changing ends or bowlers.

preferential voting system
The voting system used in all Australian elections in which voters must state their order of preference for all candidates, from their first to their last choice.

squatters
People who settled on land belonging to the state to raise animals.

stations
Sheep or cattle farms.

swagman
Person who roams the outback in search of work.

tinnie
A can, usually of beer.

transportation
A system of punishment in which criminals and convicts, mainly from Britain and Ireland, were exiled to Australia from the late 18th to the early 19th century.

FOR FURTHER INFORMATION

BOOKS

Macintyre, Stuart. *A Concise History of Australia.* Port Melbourne, VIC, Australia: Cambridge University Press, 2009.

North, Peter. *Welcome to My Country: Australia.* London, England: Franklin Watts, 2010.

Vaisutis, Justine et al. *Lonely Planet Australia.* Footscray, VIC, Australia: Lonely Planet, 2011.

VIDEOS

Amazing Australia. VHS. America Home Treas, 2000.

Amazing Wonders of the World: Island Continent—Australia. Questar, Inc., 1999.

G'Day Australia: Like Nothing Else on Earth. Paramount Studio, 1998.

National Geographic's Australia's Great Barrier Reef. National Geographic, 2000.

DVDs

Australia to the Max. Questar, 2007.

Discovery Atlas: Australia Revealed. Discovery Channel, 2007.

Planet Earth—Australia. DVD International, 2002.

Reader's Digest: Australia the Beautiful. Questar, 2004.

BIBLIOGRAPHY

BOOKS

Central Intelligence Agency. *The CIA World Factbook*. Washington, D.C.: Central Intelligence Agency, 2011.

Horne, Donald. *The Story of the Australian People*. Sydney, Australia: Reader's Digest, 1985.

Kelly, Andrew. *Australia*. New York: Bookwright Press, 1989.

Lawson, Henry. *The Bush Undertaker and Other Stories*. Sydney, Australia: Angus & Robertson, 1970.

Luling, Virginia. *Aborigines*. Englewood Cliffs, NJ: Silver Burdett, 1979.

Nicholson, Margaret. *The Little Aussie Fact Book*. Camberwell, VIC, Australia: Penguin Australia, 2000.

Stark, Al. *Australia: A Lucky Land*. Minneapolis, MN: Dillon, 1987.

WEBSITES

About Australia. www.about-australia.com

Australia Online. www.australia-online.com

Australian Bureau of Statistics. www.abs.gov.au

Department of Foreign Affairs and Trade. www.dfat.gov.au

Lonely Planet World Guide: Destination Australia. www.lonelyplanet.com/australia

Official site of the Australian Tourist Commission. www.australia.com

INDEX

INDEX